FLIGHTS OF INSPIRATION

Michael D. Britten

AuthorHouse™ UK Ltd.
500 Avebury Boulevard
Central Milton Keynes, MK9 2BE
www.authorhouse.co.uk
Phone: 08001974150

© 2009 Michael D. Britten. All rights reserved.

No part of this book may be reproduced, stored in a retrieval system, or transmitted by any means without the written permission of the author.

First published by AuthorHouse 2/26/2009

ISBN: 978-1-4389-5223-9 (sc)

Printed in the United States of America
Bloomington, Indiana

This book is printed on acid-free paper.

Contents

Introduction 3
Preface 7
Chapter 1　Early History 13
Chapter 2　Preparing The Ground 18
Chapter 3　On A Wing And A Prayer 24
Chapter 4　The Aerial Cowboy 28
Chapter 6　Another Beginning 33
Chapter 6　Flying Colours 37
Chapter 7　The First Casualties 41
Chapter 8　A Very Different Pioneer 46
Chapter 9　The Navy Gets Airborne 52
Chapter 10　Gordon Bennett ! 57
Chapter 11　Soldiers, Sailors And Airmen 69
Chapter 12　Lights Out 73
Chapter 13　Evacuation 79
Chapter 14　Uncles 82
Chapter 15　Sleeping Quarters 86
Chapter 16　Under Fire 90
Chapter 17　Short Shrift For Shorts 94
Chapter 18　The Stranger 98
Chapter 19　Over The Pond 103
Chapter 20　All Aboard 110
Chapter 21　Touch Down 114
Chapter 22　Reverse Gear 118
Chapter 23　Full Circle 124
Chapter 24　That's Entertainment 130
Chapter 25　Shooting Stars 136
Chapter 26　Marooned 147
Chapter 27　Without The Crowds 151
Chapter 28　Artistic Licence 155
Chapter 29　Cockles And Mussels 159
Chapter 30　Going Underground 163
Chapter 31　The Shirt 168
Chapter 32　Ground To Air Missiles 172

Chapter 33 Time Bomb 176
Chapter 34 Career Options 181
Chapter 37 The Great Flood 185
Chapter 36 Cash And Carry 190
Chapter 37 Moving On 195
Chapter 38 Bombs Away 199
Chapter 39 Quality Leisure Time 204
Chapter 40 Two Red Cards 209
Chapter 41 Blue Eyed Boy 219
Chapter 42 In Memoriam 225
Chapter 43 The Sinking Of The Flying Boat 230
Chapter 44 White Elephants 234
Chapter 45 From First To Last 239
Chapter 46 Three Or Four ? 243
Chapter 47 Opportunity Knocks 247
Author's Personal Details: 251

INTRODUCTION

Halfway along the North Kent coast some fifty miles from Central London lies an island that the modern world has left behind.

It takes its name from the sheep that have for centuries grazed its marshland and it has only one town of any consequence. The remainder of its inhabitants live along a low ridge overlooking the ever-widening expanse of the Thames Estuary.

The islanders, numbering nearly 40,000, are known as "swampies", originally a term of derision, but now affectionately regarded as a badge of identity. Indulging in nostalgia is one of their favourite pastimes.

Until 1860 the island could be reached only by boat across the sea inlet that divides it from the rest of the 'Garden of England.' Tolls to use the King's Ferry were not abolished until 1929, and during two World Wars it was a restricted area, closed to the outside world because of its military installations.

Its legacy of those hostilities lies a mile offshore in the swirling grey waters of what used to be called the German Ocean, in the form of a boatload of American munitions that foundered on a sandbank in 1944. No one is sure whether its deteriorating cargo is harmless, or constitutes a lethal threat to life and property.

Today the Isle of Sheppey is a poor relation to its prosperous neighbours, the towns of Sittingbourne and Faversham ,with which it makes up the administrative borough of Swale. Old industries have died and not been replaced. Starved of investment and modern facilities, it is desperately in need of regeneration

Yet it was the cradle of aviation in the British Isles. It was here that the first flight by a Briton was made from the Royal Aero Club's first airfield, close to Muswell Manor near the village of Leysdown. Nearby Eastchurch saw the birth of the seaplane and the Royal Naval Air Service.

The summer of 2009 marks the centenary of that first manned flight. Unlike the island, the exploits of those magnificent men in their flying machines are in no danger of being forgotten.

This is the tale of those pioneers who gave us all a big lift, coupled with the personal and family memories of a writer who grew up where history was made in the first half of the 20th Century.

PREFACE

In the Spring of 1961, a chance meeting with a distinguished Peer of the Realm, gave me the idea for this book. That it has taken so long to come to fruition is due more to a surfeit of personal procrastination, than consideration of its relationship to the calendar.

Despite the long delay it remains an inspirational story, and now with centenary celebrations approaching, the opportunity has arrived to relate his major, and my family's exceedingly minor, part in the history of British aviation.

The encounter came in the very early days of my career as a sports journalist when the Professional Golfers Association of Great Britain and Ireland held a press conference at their headquarters inside the Oval cricket ground.

It concerned that year's Ryder Cup match against the USA. The biennial Golf contest would in future be decided over 24 matches rather than 12; there would be four foursomes and eight singles on each of the two days; and all games would be over 18 holes instead of 36. The Americans had agreed to the new format, and it would be introduced at the forthcoming encounter at Royal Lytham and St Anne's.

It was customary for officials to dispense refreshments after such announcements and mingle with the Press contingent. Also present were players like Dai Rees, captain of the victorious GB and Ireland team in 1957, Bernard Hunt and Neil Coles.

While I was trying to keep a low profile in that august company, I was approached by a vaguely familiar elderly figure, who I recognised as part of the official party. He asked me where I came from.

Misunderstanding the enquiry, I replied " I come from a little village in Kent which I doubt you have ever heard of ." He responded : "Try me" .

When I mentioned Leysdown-on-Sea he said " Oh yes, it is at the far end of the Isle of Sheppey and it has a public house called the Rose and Crown. That's where it all began." Seeing my surprise he added "Look me up, and you will understand."

It did not take me long to discover that he was the President of the PGA of Great Britain and Ireland, and that the new Ryder Cup format had been his idea.

He was of course the first Lord Brabazon of Tara, one of the pioneers of aviation, who after an outstanding career in politics ,had become hugely influential in the golf world in his later years. He was well known for the authorship of a Government report that led to the establishment of today's British airline industry, and a giant airliner that bore his name.

But the principal reason he will always remain in my memory is for what he achieved as a daring young man on the fields of Sheppey, where I grew up in the public house in which he once supped a celebratory ale.

He had a high old time there, as did I in my formative years. He and his fellow pioneers were responsible for making the world a smaller place , and I owe him the same debt as the many millions who have strapped themselves into the seat of an airliner, and soared off to faraway places. Nowadays we regard such travel as routine. A century ago we would have been as petrified as the piglet he took to the skies over Sheppey

In the following chapters, devoted chiefly to those magnificent men in their flying machines, I have also drawn on personal and family experiences to show what it was like growing up in an ageing community that had embraced a rich history. Yet one that was suspicious of change, and reluctant to give youth a voice. One where the most desirable things always seemed to be elsewhere.

Acknowledgements:

For the invaluable assistance of the following I am most grateful:

Dennis and Daphne Arnold
Bel Austin
Sharon and Terry Munns
Sheerness Times Guardian

Michael D. Britten

For Jenny, Bill, Calum and Harry.

Chapter 1
EARLY HISTORY

The recorded history of the Isle of Sheppey dates back to the Romans who called it *insula ovium*. It is likely that Caesar's men simply waded ashore this large expanse of low-lying sheep pasture, and marched to the highest point at Minster, some 250 feet above sea level.

There they pitched camp and constructed a pagan temple, probably dedicated to Apollo. Roman coins and artefacts have been found by archaeologists in the area of the subsequent Saxon-built Minster Abbey and Benedictine monastery that were constructed in the seventh century.

Evidently, judging from the Bronze Age relics also discovered, this had been an important religious site from prehistoric times. It really came to prominence in 675 AD when the widowed Kentish queen Sexburga became its first abbess. She was canonised for using water from its Holy Healing Well, mixing it with herbs to 'effect magical cures in peoples and animals'.

Her sister, daughter, and grand-daughter all became abbesses of this establishment for nuns of 'high and noble birth', and were duly canonised as Saints Werburga, Etheldreda, and Erminhilda.

The Saxons called the island *Sceapige* which is the derivation of the word sheep, and translates to the modern Sheppey, while the name Minster derives from the Latin *monasterium*, denoting the site of a monastery or abbey.

However the Saxons were under constant threat of invasion, and the Danes twice succeeded in establishing their rule, firstly in 798, and then again, according to the Anglo Saxon Chronicles, in 832. By 855 the Danes had establishment permanent control, which lasted until Earl Godwin, father of King Harold, drove them out in 1052, destroying Minster Abbey in the process.

The Norman Conquest of 1066 brought a long period of stability. Minster Abbey was rebuilt and a parish church added. In the middle of the 13th Century there was another burst of ecclesiastical fervour, and churches were constructed at Eastchurch, Leysdown, and isolated Harty from where a ferry crossed the Swale and gave access to Faversham.

Flights of Inspiration

Queenborough Castle was built in 1366 by Edward III, and 20 years later his grandson Richard II ordered coastal defences to be constructed. A programme of road improvements was begun in 1406 by Henry IV who introduced tolls on the principal ferry to and from the mainland.

Royalty continued to be associated with Sheppey for Queen Elizabeth I became Lady of the Manor of Shurland in 1582, and there is widespread belief that Henry VIII and Anne Boleyn spent their honeymoon at the now ruined Shurland Hall in 1532-3.

Certainly Henry knew all about the island, for the Dissolution of the Monasteries accounted for the sale of Minster Abbey to one of his favourites in 1539, and he was responsible for bringing the port of Sheerness into existence by ordering the construction of a fort to protect the entrance to the River Medway.

Indications that Sheppey's allegiance had switched to the Parliamentarians in the English Civil War are apparent from the fact that Sir Michael Livesay, who resided at Parsonage Farm, Eastchurch, and Augustine Garland, the MP for the 'rotten borough' of Queenborough, were two of the signatories to the death warrant of King Charles I, executed in January 1649.

Both paid the price for their temerity on the Restoration of Charles II in 1660. Livesay was hunted down and murdered after fleeing to Holland, while Garland was sold into slavery.

Five years later Navy Secretary Samuel Pepys marked out the site for a dockyard and fortified garrison at Sheerness, but work did not begin until 1669, two years after a Dutch squadron under Admiral de Ruyter, sailed boldly into the mouth of the Medway. Henry VIII's fort proved totally inadequate in withstanding the Dutch cannon and was destroyed.

The Dutch came ashore and occupied the Isle of Sheppey taking 4000 sheep, but apparently none of the women, which says much for the quality of the flocks. Then they sailed further up the river towards the Royal Dockyard at Chatham, demolishing Upnor Castle, and all but destroying an English fleet at anchor. They captured its flagship the Royal Charles, causing panic in London. Not surprisingly this shameful episode has traditionally been under-reported in British history books.

A cholera epidemic afflicted the island in 1834, but throughout the 19th Century improvements to the Dockyard were made, better communications established, and local and district councils formed.

The first bridge joining Sheppey to the mainland was constructed in 1860, bringing the railway from Sittingbourne, and in 1902 the Sheppey Light Railway, linking the eastern village of Leysdown to Sheerness East and Queenborough, was opened.

The first decade of the 20th Century saw Sheppey become the cradle of British aviation. The first recorded flight by a Briton on British soil was made by John Brabazon at the first British airfield. Aircraft production was begun by the Short brothers, initially at Shell Beach near Leysdown, subsequently at Eastchurch. The modern era had begun.

Chapter 2
PREPARING THE GROUND

One mile east of Leysdown stands Muswell Manor, a substantial 16th Century house in extensive grounds. In 1909 it became the first headquarters of the Royal Aero Club, with an airfield at nearby Shell Beach.

This organisation had been formed eight years earlier by wealthy motorists Frank Hedges Butler, his daughter Vera, and the Hon. Charles Rolls, a well-connected young aristocrat, who had gained a masters degree in engineering at Trinity College, Cambridge.

Rolls was the third son of Lord Llangattock, who had been Conservative MP for Monmouth from 1880-85. Born in Berkeley Square, he had been educated at Eton before going to University, where as an 18 year old undergraduate he acquired his first automobile.

He had a Peugeot machine imported from France, only to be told by police when it arrived that he needed a man with a red flag to walk ahead of him, and that he must not exceed four mph. It took Rolls over 12 hours to get the car to Cambridge, where he immediately launched a successful campaign to get the speed limit raised to 12 mph.

Rolls ,who stood an imposing 6ft 5ins, was firstly a racing cyclist before his love of speed led him to racing automobiles with his friend John Brabazon, and the pair became enthusiastic balloonists. When in December 1903 the American Wright Brothers, Orville and Wilbur, became the world's first airmen by taking off from the sands of Kitty Hawk in North Carolina, Rolls became impatient to learn about powered flight.

He had already met Henry Royce in Manchester and they had agreed to the formation of a luxury motor car company, henceforth to be known as Rolls-Royce. While Henry would design the engine and build the cars, the extrovert Rolls would demonstrate and sell them.

It was while he was at the New York motor show in 1906, to which he had gone to promote the company's new Silver Ghost model, that Rolls attended an American Aero Club demonstration, and met Wilbur and Orville Wright.

Rolls urged them to visit Europe and demonstrate the aircraft they had produced at their Ohio factory in late 1905. After taking the precaution of registering their patents, they did so in 1908 and 1909, initially with the intention of selling their designs to European Governments. When that did not materialise, the two Americans licensed certain European manufacturers to copy their designs.

The Short brothers, Horace, Eustace, and Oswald, who were friends of Rolls and built balloons for the Aero Club, were among those who were granted a licence to produce 'Wright Flyers'.

In the meantime Gabriel Voisin, a contemporary French aviator, was well on the way to producing his own aeroplane. Gabriel and his brother Charles had established a factory at Billancourt on the western outskirts of Paris in 1907. Within a year they were making planes to order.

Brabazon, who along with several other British aviators had attended the Wright demonstrations in France, also visited the Voisin factory. He learnt to fly there, and purchased one of Voisin's biplanes which he had shipped back to England.

Muswell, or Mussel Manor as it was then known, had been spotted as a promising site for the Aero Club's operations by balloonist Griffith Brewer. Soaring overhead, he took note of a wide area of unobstructed grassland that was within easy reach of London, and was served by road and the newly-created Sheppey Light Railway which terminated at Leysdown.

It was just what Eustace and Oswald Short were looking for. They had become hooked on aviation in 1897, when they made their maiden flight in a second-hand coal gas balloon which they had bought for £30. Eustace was 22 at the time, and Oswald was just 14.

They began manufacturing balloons above a laboratory run by their elder brother Horace in Hove, before moving to London and setting up operations underneath railway arches at Battersea, from where they supplied Aero Club members.

Persuaded by Rolls, they too had seen the Wright demonstrations in Paris, and in November 1908 had convinced Horace, who had been working on steam turbines in Newcastle, that he should join them in a new venture to make aeroplanes. Horace's first contribution was to travel to France and obtain a precious licence for the fledgling Short Brothers company to build six 'Wright Flyers' for members of the Aero Club, two of which were ordered by Rolls.

The Shorts had already leased the land from its owner, local builder James Andrews, and at the end of January 1909 had started bringing their workers down from London to build construction sheds and storage facilities at neighbouring Shell Beach, near the hamlet of Shellness. The wealthy McClean, who was to become the principal benefactor of the Short company, and later its chief test pilot, had simultaneously leased the Manor and a further 400 acres for the use of the Aero Club

On May 4th 1909 a veritable Who's Who of aviation pioneers converged on Mussel Manor. Rolls drove the Wright Brothers there in his personal Silver Ghost, to join Horace, Eustace, and Oswald Short, and John Brabazon, as well as other Aero Club notables such as Francis McClean, Griffith Brewer, and founder member Frank Hedges Butler.

Brabazon's Voisin aircraft had already been reassembled in the new Shorts workshops, and preparations had begun for his first flight on British soil. It bore little resemblance to the streamlined machines with which we are so familiar today. It looked like an enormous box kite on wheels with its engine behind an open cockpit, reflecting the experiments the Voisin brothers had carried out on the River Seine, where they had towed their prototype kites behind a motor boat.

John Theodore Cuthbert Moore-Brabazon, to give him his full name, had named his craft *Bird of Passage*. There had been several weeks of practice take offs which could only be undertaken when conditions were favourable and the wind was in the right direction. Brabazon had whiled away many hours in shooting on the marshes or playing golf on a rudimentary course nearby.

On May 2 the weather was deemed ideal and his machine was wheeled from its hangar to prepare for lift off. The first two attempts were failures, but the third saw *Bird of Passage* soar to a maximum height of 40 feet, travelling some 500 yards before coming down to earth. This event was officially recognised as the first flight in Britain by a British aviator, and Brabazon was awarded the Aero Club's pilot certificate number one.

Chapter 3
ON A WING AND A PRAYER

John Brabazon was by no means content to rest on his laurels, but he needed to take stock before embarking on a long and distinguished career in aviation.

Although he had proved the Voisin, which had a top speed of 40 mph, could fly, it had severe limitations. It could travel only in a straight line because its simple elevator and elementary rudder controls made it almost impossible to make turns. Additionally it did not meet the stipulations laid down for his next challenge. The Daily Mail newspaper had offered a first prize of £1,000 to the first Briton to fly a circular mile over British soil, but it had to be achieved in an all-British built machine.

Brabazon gave the order to Shorts to build him a Wright Flyer in their new Leysdown workshops at a cost of £1500. A total of £400 went on the engine, another

Flights of Inspiration

£400 had to be paid under the licence agreement to the Wright brothers, while Shorts retained the balance.

By the end of September it had been delivered to Brabazon who moved into Mussel Manor along with a reporter from the newspaper, while he made his preparations. His first flight in May had been witnessed by only a handful of Aero Club members. This time word had got out, partly because of the newspaper's promotional activities, and partly because some of the key Shorts workers were billeted at the Rose and Crown public house in nearby Leysdown.

Curious villagers were continually strolling along the beach to see what was happening at the airfield and when, on the 30th October 1909, Brabazon decided that conditions were perfect for his attempt on the circular mile, a sizeable crowd had gathered on the shingle ridge leading to Shellness.

On his first attempt his new Wright Flyer crashed on take off. Horace Short was summoned to effect emergency repairs , and a few hours later Brabazon was ready to try again.

At the second attempt he took off from close to Shorts factory, headed in the direction of the Manor and completed a circle of more than one and a half miles at an average height of 20 feet in a time of two minutes 36 seconds.

The Aero Club and the Daily Mail reporter, who rejoiced in his major scoop, verified the feat, and Brabazon was awarded the prize. He later reckoned it had cost him more than £2,500 to win £1,000, but it was an observation not a complaint, and he bought himself a commemorative cup from his winnings.

Six days later Brabazon was in the air again, making the flamboyant gesture for which he became renowned. There are conflicting reports as to the exact circumstances. Some onlookers were convinced that he had heard someone in the crowd, watching his successful circular mile, remark that he has as much chance of doing it as a pig had of flying.

Brabazon said in his memoirs " a local farmer suggested I might take a pig up with me and so accomplish what had been proverbially impossible. So I went to Leysdown and secured one."

What is not in doubt is that it was acquired for him by Jim Pankhurst, who was gardener and potman at the Rose and Crown at that time, at a cost of ten shillings. Pankhurst and his wife were well known to the aviators at Muswell Manor, for she often supplied them with hot meals and drinks.

Brabazon had a waste-paper basket fastened to a strut on his port wing, and strapped the small pig inside. On the outside of the basket was a handwritten notice which said "I am the first pig to fly".

He named the animal ICARUS II after the Greek myth which describes how the son of Daedalus ignored his father's advice and flew too close to the Sun, causing the wax in his wings to melt, and him to drown in the sea.

After landing Brabazon reported " although he squealed a bit to begin with he soon settled down and was not the slightest distressed. When we landed he showed not the slightest desire to depart, and waddled behind the aircraft as it was taken back to the hangar".

The pig's reward was to be sold to a Mr Harris, the so-called "Sausage Man" for the sum of £5, on the understanding that it would be used only for "publicity purposes".

By the end of the year Brabazon had scooped another £1,000 prize, on that occasion presented by the Michelin brothers, for the first long distance flight in British aviation. He covered a distance of 17 miles.

Chapter 4
THE AERIAL COWBOY

Brabazon was not the first man to take to the air in Britain. That honour went on October 16, 1908 to Samuel Franklin Cody, an American who had first made his name by touring the country with his Wild West Show.

Samuel Cody was no relation to William Frederick Cody, otherwise known as "Buffalo Bill" , the former Pony Express rider, US Army scout, and buffalo hunter. Yet he claimed to be his son, borrowed his name, and adopted his persona.

Both were born in Iowa, Bill Cody in 1846, and Samuel in 1861 where his surname was registered as Cowdery. Samuel later claimed that he had trained as a cowboy, hunted buffalo, and had been a prospector in the Yukon during the Klondike Gold Rush. How much was fact, or the product of a lively imagination, has never been satisfactorily established. What is known, is that he had changed his name to Cody by the time he began touring the USA with his show, in which he was billed as the King of the Cowboys.

He married Maud Maria Lee in Pennsylvania in 1889, using the name of Cody, and both appeared in his version of life in the American West which he brought to Europe, the following year. The authentic Cody was also touring the USA and Europe around this time, with sharpshooter Annie Oakley and the Indian chief Sitting Bull, among his entourage. Buffalo Bill was presented by the publicists as the Prince of the Plains.

Inevitably the appearance of two Codys presenting similar Wild West Shows, caused widespread confusion, which Samuel encouraged by growing a similar beard, moustache, and shoulder length hair to that sported by Bill.

Not long after he reached Britain he dumped his wife in favour of another woman named Elizabeth King, who along with her two children, took his adopted surname, and Maria's part in the show when she returned to the USA.

Sometime in the early 1890's Samuel Cody became interested in kites. He built and tested them, and when he produced a large box-kite with a basket slung underneath that could carry one or two men up to heights of over

1000 feet, he offered it to the War Office for spotting during the Boer War.

Then, with an ever-open eye for a spot of self-publicity, he crossed the English Channel in a boat towed by one of his kites.

The Admiralty became interested in his experiments, and in September 1908 he launched another of his observation kites off a warship at Portsmouth. Cody's wooing of the Navy came to an abrupt end when he overplayed his hand, asking for too much money.

Before long the Army had hired him as Chief Instructor in Kiting at the Balloon School in Aldershot at a salary of £1000 per annum. Cody formed two Kite sections of the Royal Engineers which became the Air Battalion of the RE. In 1907 he was involved in the construction of Britain's first Army airship.

It flew from Aldershot to London with Cody on board, circled St Paul's Cathedral, then set out on the return journey, before high winds resulted in an emergency landing having to be made . The airship was damaged, and this incident helped to persuade the War Office, representing both the Army and the Navy, that there was no future for airships and planes.

Undaunted, Cody moved on from experiments with gliders, to begin developing his own aircraft at

Flights of Inspiration

Farnborough. With financial help from the Army he was able to complete construction, and began testing British Army Aeroplane No 1 in September 1908. At first it was just a matter of short hops, then on October 16, 1908 he flew a distance of some 460 yards.

Although he was in the air for only 30 seconds, this flight was announced, and recognised, as the first by a heavier than air machine in the British Isles, a full 197 days before Brabazon's take off at Muswell Manor.

On June 7th 1910 Samuel Cody was awarded the Royal Aero Club's certificate No 9, and the following month took up a passenger, his former co-pilot in the Army airship, before making a cross-country flight of more than an hour. He was awarded the Royal Aero Club's coveted Gold Medal in 1912.

He continued with his pioneering work, and by the summer of 1913 was a public hero. His extraordinary life came to an end on August 7th when he was joy-riding with a passenger in a newly-designed float plane. It broke up at 500 feet and both were killed.

Cody was buried with full military honours at Aldershot and his funeral attracted a crowd of 100,000. His memory lives on in the form of a full size replica of the British Army No 1 plane , the "Fast Cody Flyer" which has been on show at the Farnborough Museum since October 2008, when the Centenary of the United Kingdom's first powered flight was celebrated.

The two Kite sections of the Royal Engineers, which Cody had formed nearly a decade earlier, were subsequently designated No 1 Squadron of the Royal Flying Corps, and finally No 1 Squadron of the Royal Air Force when it came into being on April 1st 1918.

Chapter 6
ANOTHER BEGINNING

About the same time as John Brabazon was creating history by getting his heavier-than-air machine to take off at Leysdown in 1909, Percival Clarke was sweeping Maud Barnwell off her feet on the North West Frontier.

He was a lance-bombardier in the 86th Heavy Artillery Regiment, while she was an ayah, or nursemaid, to the children of one of his officers. Both were coming to the end of their periods of service in India, where they had met at a hill station to which soldiers were periodically sent to escape the fierce summer heat.

Their marriage took place at Rawalpindi, in what is now northern Pakistan, and after a brief honeymoon they were soon on the boat that brought them back to Southampton. Percy duly secured his release papers and the newly-weds headed for London where he was due to begin a new career in the Metropolitan police. He was 23, she a year younger.

Maud was strikingly pretty with cornflower blue eyes, just like her Irish-born mother Barbara, who had unwittingly been the cause of her presence in the sub-Continent. Barbara, who hailed from County Meath, was the reason why Maud's father Charles, one of the sons of a wealthy London businessman, had been disowned by his parents and become financially embarrassed.

The Barnfield family were not socially superior, they were in fact sweeps. However their sphere of operation was the West End, principally the whole of Mayfair, where they owned chimney-sweeping concessions for all the best addresses. It was a dirty, but extremely lucrative business, providing sufficient income for them to live well in one of the choicest residential areas.

Charles had met Barbara some 20 years after her penniless family had emigrated to London in the aftermath of the series of potato famines that afflicted Ireland during the middle of the 19th Century. There were rumours that she was the illegitimate product of a liaison between a member of the Irish gentry and a housemaid. No proof was discovered, but when Charles announced his intention to wed her, he was told he would forfeit his inheritance if he married "beneath his station". Fortunately for me, love triumphed, and he duly became the black sheep of the Barnfield family.

Flights of Inspiration

Ostracism was confirmed when in 1887 Barbara gave birth to Maud, the first of three girls for whom career prospects were limited in Victorian society. Like her siblings Maud was destined to go into service, in her case child care.

My grandparents settled in the East End on their return from India, starting their family with Cyril in 1910, and Barbara my mother in 1913. Sadly Cyril was an early victim of diptheria, and a second son Alec arrived in 1917.

My mother was born in Whitechapel, well within the sound of Bow Bells, which is still the qualification for a genuine Cockney. After the First World War the family moved south of the Thames to where Maud's sisters lived in a large rented Victorian property at Nunhead, near Peckham Rye.

The open spaces of the common were a welcome relief from the smoke and grime of the inner city, and Barbara excelled as a teenage athlete, winning London Schools sprint titles as a 15 year old. Her first employment was as a clerk in the offices of the Jones and Higgins department store in Peckham High Road, where she later trained as a shorthand typist.

That was the era of the Charleston, and Barbara was an enthusiastic devotee when the craze hit Britain. It was at a local dance hall that the vivacious 21 year old met

Herbert Britten, a long distance lorry driver from New Cross.

He was one of the "knights of the road" of the years between the two World Wars, paid the then princely sum of £3.50 per week to transport goods from the docks at Bermondsey and Rotherhithe to all parts of the country. He knew the A6, and the long haul over Shap summit to Scotland, like the back of his hand. "Bert" was also a first-rate vehicle mechanic.

They married in 1935, and there was enough money for them to move out to the leafy suburbs. They set up home in a rented bungalow in Bexley, close enough for Bert to reach dockland via the Dover to London road within half an hour.

On the other side of the trunk road lay the small town of Bexleyheath At a nursing home sited at 315 The Broadway I struggled into this world shortly after 11.00 pm on Saturday March 13th , 1937.

A little more than two years later, as two trains of evacuee children headed from Sheppey to Wales and the West Country, I went in the opposite direction to become one of the youngest "swampies" in the hill-top village of Minster, astride the road from Sheerness to Leysdown.

Chapter 6
FLYING COLOURS

Although Rolls had been pipped at the post by Brabazon in the race to become the first Briton aloft, it was not long before he caught up and overtook his great rival.

He had been forced to wait his turn for the first of his Wright Flyer machines because the first two had been reserved for Frank McClean and Brabazon. Then when Rolls did take possession he ran into the same problems as the others in making a safe take off and landing on the uneven ground at Muswell Manor.

The problem of the many hollows on the marshland was resolved when one of Shorts' workers had the idea of burning the grass in the depressions so that they could easily be seen from the air, and thus avoided when landing. The difficulties in navigating the numerous drainage ditches, prior to take off. were solved by an ingenious catapult-launching arrangement.

A piece of rail some 100 feet long was positioned to face into the wind, and the aircraft was mounted on a crossbar straddled across the monorail. At the rear of the rail a pylon was built, and up to half a ton of weights was hoisted to the top. Then a stout rope was attached to the weights over pulleys, before being taken over the machine to a point halfway down the rail. From there it was relayed over another pulley wheel and back to the front of the crossbar and aeroplane.

The theory was that when the pilot was ready to take off with engine running, he released a catch . The weights began to drop rapidly, and the machine was propelled along the rail at sufficient speed to lift it into the air.

In practice it was a hazardous experience, as Rolls' chauffeur and general factotum T.O.Smith graphically illustrated when his employer made his first attempt. He said "having got everything ready, the engine started and then the final let-go, the machine careered along the rail at what seemed a terrific speed. When it reached the end of the rail it suddenly shot straight up into the air, and a second later crashed down on its tail with a terrific bang.

"We found Mr Rolls getting out of the mess, fortunately unhurt. He said 'this is my first lesson. I am afraid I gave the elevator too much lift, but better luck next time."

The wreckage was returned to the Shorts factory in a horse and cart, but before long Rolls had mastered this take off technique, and was soon regularly reaching heights of 60 feet, the best yet achieved at Muswell Manor.

However the difficulties of the Shell Beach terrain were clearly dangerous to would-be flyers, and the search began for a more suitable home for both the Aero Club and the Shorts Factory. An extensive survey of the island resulted in a site at Eastchurch being chosen, and the wealthy McClean bought Stonepitts Farm at the foot of Standford Hill, leasing it to the Aero Club at a peppercorn rent of one shilling per annum.

Before long the Shorts brothers, their factory sheds and hangars, and their workforce of 80 men had left Leysdown for good, and by May 1910 were established at Eastchurch. They had completed their contract to build the six Wright Flyers and had decided not to renew it, because they considered the American design had become obsolete. The three brothers were confident they could develop their own designs, and build superior aircraft.

Rolls had been the first to land on the new 25 acres site at Eastchurch, back in November 1909, and he continued his flying training by towing a glider up Standford Hill behind his distinctive white Silver Ghost. By the end of the year he had flown distances up to 15 miles and was awarded the Aero club's pilot certificate number two. Both he and Brabazon were presented with these in the Spring of 1910. For the rest of his life Brabazon's car bore the registration FLY 1.

Yet British aviators were still a long way behind their Continental cousins. In July 1909 Louis Bleriot had become the first to fly the Channel and other Frenchmen like the Voisin brothers, Henri Farman, Louis Breguet and Jacques de Lesseps, had made significant advances in the new science of flying heavier-than-air machines.

Rolls gained a worthy place among this elite after purchasing a French-built Wright aircraft in April 1910, and within six weeks making the first double crossing of the English Channel. On June 2, 1910 he flew from England to France and back to England in a time of 95 minutes and 30 seconds.

He was awarded the Royal Aero Club's Gold Medal, only the fourth it had issued. The first recipients were Americans Wilbur and Orville Wright, then the Frenchman Bleriot.

Chapter 7
THE FIRST CASUALTIES

Rolls had won great public acclaim for his Channel double but his triumph was short-lived. Just over a month later he was killed in a flying accident during an air show to celebrate the town of Bournemouth's centenary.

A French-built tail plane had been fitted to his Wright aircraft , in what was deemed an unapproved modification, and it broke off in a 20-25 mph wind. The plane flipped over and crashed, and although Rolls was only 20 feet above the ground his skull was shattered.

His achievements had made him a national hero, to such an extent that Lord Montague of Beaulieu interrupted his speech in the House of Lords to announce his death. Rolls was Britain's first aircraft fatality , at the age of 33. His demise so saddened John Brabazon that he grounded himself, and did not fly again until the outbreak of World War One in 1914.

It was also a grievous blow to the Royal Aero Club pioneers, and it was quickly followed by another when the equally cavalier Cecil Grace, who had flown with Rolls on a circular tour of Sheppey early in 1910, was lost at sea.

Grace, who had been born in Chile, was the nephew of a former Mayor of New York. He had graduated from Columbia University, and had gone up to Oxford when his parents came to live in Britain. In April 1910 he had drawn attention to himself and the military possibilities of aircraft, by making a reconnaissance of a fleet of British warships anchored off Sheerness.

He startled its officers by suddenly appearing out of a mist and manoeuvring overhead at various heights, before soaring up to 1500 feet and disappearing in the general direction of Eastchurch, from where he had taken off.

In December he attempted to beat a newly established record by Tommy Sopwith, a rival in the Baron de Forest challenge for a long distance flight by a Briton in a British machine to the Continent. On the 22nd he took off for Belgium, but strong winds forced him down at Sangatte, near Calais. In attempting to make the return trip the following evening, he took off into a thick fog, but never made landfall. He was last seen over the Goodwin Sands, heading in the direction of the North Sea.

Flights of Inspiration

Despite an intensive search of the English Channel, and the remotest parts of East Anglia, there was no trace of him or his aircraft, until some weeks later a flying cap and a pair of goggles were fished out of the sea, close to where some wreckage was discovered off the Belgian coast.

These setbacks did not however halt flying activity at Eastchurch. While Shorts concentrated on aircraft manufacture, the Aero Club, which had acquired its Royal prefix earlier in the year, pressed ahead with training its members, as well as other would-be aviators eager to obtain one of their coveted pilot's licences.

This was by no means an easy task, for training could only take place when the winds were light, which was usually in the early morning or late evening. If the wind speed topped 10 mph, training flights were banned for safety reasons. Early learners had to crouch behind the instructor and grip the controls when ordered. It was not until Shorts produced two-seater planes with dual controls, that training became more comfortable.

One of the earliest "freelance" pupils was Naval lieutenant George Colmore, who learnt to fly at his own expense, going solo on June 21st to gain pilot certificate number 15.

The 31st pilot to gain his flying certificate was T.OM. Sopwith who achieved lasting fame as a manufacturer and went on to become "the grand old man of British aviation." Christened Thomas Octave Murdoch, but thereafter always known as "Tommy", Sopwith went solo on October 22, and on December 18th won the De Forest prize by flying from Eastchurch to Thirlemont in Belgium, a distance of 169 miles, in three hours 40 minutes. It was this feat that the hapless Grace lost his life in trying to surpass.

Sopwith used his £4000 prize money to set up a flying school at Brooklands, but it was as an aircraft manufacturer that he excelled after setting up his Aviation Company in a disused skating rink in Kingston-on-Thames. It produced the renowned Sopwith Pup and Camel single seat fighter, of which there were more than 5,700 in the total of 18,000 aircraft he turned out for the Royal Flying Corps during World War One.

He was awarded the CBE in 1918, only to be faced with bankruptcy after the Government instituted a punitive tax on war profits. Sopwith, and his Australian test pilot Harry Hawker, formed a new company Hawker Aviation, which subsequently became Hawker Siddeley, and was responsible for the Hurricane, Typhoon, and Tempest fighters of World War Two.

Sopwith was also an outstanding yachtsman, and challenged for the Americas Cup in 1934 and 1937 in his own boats which he helmed. He was knighted in 1953, and after relinquishing the chairmanship of

Hawker Siddeley when it was nationalised, continued as a consultant well into old age. On his 100th birthday he enjoyed the rare distinction of a fly-past over his home, but died the following year in 1989.

Chapter 8
A VERY DIFFERENT PIONEER

Another lance-bombardier in the Royal Artillery was to leave an indelible mark on the Isle of Sheppey after he left the Army in 1919.

Charlie Arnold arrived in Leysdown in 1934 and was to spend more than 30 years there, becoming a major figure in the transformation of the sleepy, rural village into a holiday magnet for Londoners.

A Londoner himself, he was one of 12 children of a hard-drinking Hansom cab driver who lived in Islington, now a fashionable suburb for the intelligentsia, but one of the poorest areas of the capital at the end of the 19th Century. He left school at 12, running errands for a few pennies, and tending to the horse that pulled the local rag and bone man's cart.

Flights of Inspiration

In November 1912, when he was 19, he joined the Territorial Army because it paid young men the princely sum of £12 if they undertook two weeks training each year, together with monthly drill weekends. The money helped to feed and clothe his brothers and sisters.

Early in 1914 he was called up to join the British Expeditionary Force as an ostler in charge of the horses which drew the Royal Artillery's gun carriages. He fought at the Battle of Mons, and on the Somme through 1916, before becoming a physical training instructor of new recruits at Aldershot for the final two years of the Great War.

They were hard times, both in France and Belgium, and at home. For Charlie they got a lot harder after he had married his childhood sweetheart Emma Moore following demobilisation. Their first child Stanley lived only 24 hours, the tiny baby suffering convulsions doctors could not halt. Then their next child, daughter Irene ,died of scarlet fever when she was only two years old.

Twins Dennis and Eileen arrived in January 1923, and fortunately survived to live long and fruitful lives, as did Charlie, who was 93 when he passed on in 1986. His progress from rags to relative riches had more than a flavour of the inspiration provided by the aviation pioneers.

Charlie's business career began when he and Emma took possession of a general store in the South London suburb of Plumstead. In the early days there was rarely enough money to pay the rent, or the merchants from whom they purchased their stock, let alone bear the burden of credit they felt obliged to offer the poorest of the corner shop's customers. But they survived, and by the late 1920's Charlie was able to afford a small car which they used for weekend family excursions.

It was on one such Sunday outing that Charlie discovered the delights of Leysdown and the Isle of Sheppey, albeit by accident. His intended destination was Allhallows on the Isle of Grain, but he missed the turning off the A2 London to Dover trunk road. Unwilling to retrace his steps, he decided to take the next left exit, and ended up on Sheppey at the Cowstead Corner T-junction. The left turn led to Queenborough and Sheerness. Charlie chose right and headed for Eastchurch and Leysdown.

Journey's end was the beach just beyond the village, and the lush green fields of Nutts Farm, where he got to know the owner Albert Love. The solitude, simplicity, and bracing sea air were so appealing, that before long he had sought and gained permission to pitch an ex-Army tent on the farmer's land on future visits.

Charlie subsequently sold his business in Plumstead and returned to Islington after his father had retired, to run a newsagent's premises in Essex Road. Emma had also produced their fifth child , another daughter they had named June. Her death from diptheria in 1931 just 48 hours after she had gone down into the cellar of the shop and discovered a dead rat, so sickened Charlie and Emma that they resolved to leave London at the first opportunity.

The Arnold family had by then begun to make regular weekend trips to Leysdown, and after acquiring a second-hand fairground lorry which had been converted into a primitive mobile caravan, resolved to take it there. Charlie enlisted the aid of old Army friend Bill Haley, who ran a sweet shop in Woolwich.

They hitched the lorry, which had been stripped of its engine, to the back of Charlie's car and set off at midnight one Saturday in order to avoid the attention of the Constabulary. Charlie was driving the car, while Bill was at the wheel of the lorry.

The journey passed without incident until they reached the steep, downward descent into Rochester where the heavier lorry began to catch up with Charlie's rear bumper, despite Bill's efforts to prevent a collision by hauling desperately on the handbrake. They clattered over Rochester Bridge, with Charlie 'stepping on the gas' in order to raise sufficient speed for the "convoy" to surmount the next obstacle, the ascent of Chatham Hill.

Car and lorry staggered over the crest, and from then on there were few problems as they negotiated the road through Gillingham and Rainham, before making the left turn to Sheppey and over the Kingsferry Bridge onto the island. Dawn was breaking when they reached their destination, and parked within yards of the beach on Nutts Farm.

"That was a b….. nightmare" exclaimed Bill Haley as he stepped down from the truck. "There were half a dozen times when I thought we would have a pile up." From then on, until it was broken up for scrap, the lorry-caravan sported a signboard above the cab declaring it to be "Bill Haley's Nightmare".

Charlie returned to London to fetch his family for a week's holiday, during which Farmer Love told him that the brewery which owned the nearby Rose and Crown, was looking for a new landlord, and inquired whether he would be interested. Charlie replied that he knew nothing about running a public house, but the farmer said that he felt he could "learn on the job" and offered to give him a reference.

Within a few weeks Charlie had been interviewed by brewery officials and local magistrates, who found no impediment to his adoption of the tenancy.

He arranged for his sister Lillian to take over the newsagent's shop in Islington, and early in 1934 became the new landlord of Leysdown's only hostelry. He was to remain there for the next 20 years.

Chapter 9
THE NAVY GETS AIRBORNE

Frank McClean's early support of Shorts was crucial to their development, and by the end of 1910 the brothers had built 27 planes, many of which found their way into their benefactor's private collection housed at Eastchurch.

Grace's buzzing of the fleet in the Medway had awakened the Navy to the possibilities of using aircraft to advantage, and their interest quickened when McClean offered to pay for the training of four Navy pilots, and also loan the planes. Over 200 candidates volunteered, and three lieutenants, Samson, Longmore and Gerrard, and a Royal Marines captain Gregory, were selected for the course. The most important qualifications were that they were not married, or engaged, and were willing to pay for any crashes for which they were responsible !

Flights of Inspiration

Simultaneously, Shorts began making plans to manufacture seaplanes by adding flotation bags to their land aircraft, which McClean in his capacity as the company's honorary pilot, tested on the Swale, and on the Medway at Queenborough.

The four Navy men made rapid progress in what was effectively the first Navy flying school, and by the end of 1911 a total of 19 pilots had been trained to fly, Samson being the first to go solo. On Christmas Day 1911 agreement was reached between Shorts, the Royal Aero Club, and McClean, for the Admiralty to rent the airfield for £150 per annum.

Eastchurch thus became the headquarters of the Naval wing of the Royal Flying Corps, and that led to the official formation of the Royal Naval Air Service on April 13th 1912.

Two months earlier on January 10, Lieutenant Samson had become the first airman to take off from a ship. He flew a Short biplane fitted with flotation bags, from a specially constructed wooden platform on HMS Africa, which was moored in the Medway.

In May, Samson became the first man in the world to take off from a moving vessel, when he flew the same Shorts biplane from the battleship HMS Hibernia, steaming at 10 knots in Weymouth Bay during the review of the Fleet at Spithead by King George V.

That summer also saw Winston Churchill, who had been created First Sea Lord in October 1911, taken by Brabazon to Eastchurch, where he had flying instruction. Churchill was subsequently responsible for making Eastchurch one of a ring of coastal air stations, required to protect naval installations, such as the nearby Sheerness and Chatham dockyards.

Shorts were now convinced that their future lay in the development of seaplanes, and the irrepressible McClean gave further impetus to their new strategy with a spectacular demonstration of that aircraft's capabilities.

In August 1912 he took off at 6.30 am from Harty in a Shorts seaplane fitted with floats, and headed up the Thames Estuary towards London. He flew between the bascules of Tower Bridge, then under London bridge before landing on the river, and "parking" close to Cleopatra's Needle on the Embankment.

He was apprehended of course, and ordered to taxi back to Shadwell Basin, well clear of any bridges, before attempting to make his return journey.
McClean had caused a considerable stir, and his stunt was obviously pre-meditated, because his "shooting" of Tower Bridge had been filmed and photographed.

But I do not believe it was performed in the cause of personal aggrandisement. It was much more likely that McClean was aware of the blinkered attitude of the Government towards flying. He would have known that it had rejected the Wright Brothers 1907 offer to sell their patents, and also the views of the Navy Sea Lords, who had publicly stated at the same time that they saw no place for aircraft in their sphere of operations. McClean's flamboyance was designed to show them the error of their ways.

The introduction of floats was followed by the development of folding wings, so that seaplanes could be more easily transported and stored. This came about partly because of Shorts' problems in taking seaplanes from their Eastchurch factory along the country lanes of Sheppey to the nearest stretch of suitable water for testing at Queenborough. It also meant that several aircraft could be stored on any sizeable ship. From there it was only a short step towards building a specialist vessel to carry them. Aircraft carriers were on the horizon.

Shorts realised they needed to base their operations closer to water, and began the search for suitable premises. In 1913 the company purchased eight acres of land alongside the River Medway at Rochester, and once planning approval had been secured, pushed ahead with construction of a new seaplane works.

By early 1915 the first workshop was built, as well as a concrete slipway, which enabled Shorts to launch aircraft even at low tide, and some of their workforce was transferred from Eastchurch. The business was expanding so rapidly, that McClean was unable to combine testing with his other interests. Graham Bell thus became Shorts' first professional test pilot in 1913 before handing over to Ronald Kemp, who was assisted by various freelance pilots once hostilities started the following summer. One of these was John Lankester Parker who became Chief Test Pilot in 1918 and held the post until the end of World War Two.

The second and third workshops at Rochester were completed in 1917, when Shorts moved their operations to the new seaplane headquarters. Although they maintained a presence on the island until 1934, aircraft construction at Eastchurch had effectively ended.

Chapter 10
GORDON BENNETT !

The use of the phrase Gordon Bennett is today a popular expression to signify incredulity, or disbelief, at something seen or heard. In the early part of the 20th Century it meant something totally different to racing drivers, balloonists, and pioneer aviators, particularly those at Eastchurch in 1911.

James Gordon Bennett was a real person, or rather two people, because the son had the same name as the father, who was born in Scotland then emigrated to the United States, after deciding he was not cut out to be a priest, as his Roman Catholic parents had intended. Instead he settled in Boston, and began a career in journalism that saw him launch the New York Herald newspaper in 1835, with a capital of $500, from a cellar in Wall Street. The editor's first desk was a plank resting on two barrels. In less than a year he had a daily sale of 15,000 copies.

Michael D. Britten

Gordon Bennett Jnr was born in New York in 1841, and it is because of his exploits during an astonishingly bizarre public and private life, that the expression has survived, and still flourishes.

I mention the following episodes to give those who are unaware, an inkling of the character of the man, and also the esteem, and often awe, in which he was held. As a chip off the old block, he was the poodle's plums, as one might say in polite society these days.

First he showed his yachting prowess. For his 16th birthday his father gave him a sloop named Rebecca, which he raced in the New York Yacht Club's annual cruise. Four years later, under the personal appointment of President Abraham Lincoln, he was a third lieutenant in the US Revenue Cutter Service during the American Civil War, to which the New York Herald devoted acres of newsprint, with regular reports from no less than 63 accredited correspondents.

In 1866, Bennett Senior handed over control of the newspaper to Bennett Junior, who celebrated on Christmas Day by winning the world's first trans-ocean yacht race, from New Jersey to The Needles off the Isle of Wight. He promptly became the youngest ever Commodore of the New York Yacht Club.

Three years later, he and his paper, sent Henry Morton Stanley to Africa to search for the "lost" explorer

Flights of Inspiration

David Livingstone, and the Herald had the first of many world scoops. The paper was also the first to carry news of the massacre of General Custer and his 7th cavalry by the Sioux at the Battle of the Little Big Horn in 1876.

By this time Bennett Jnr had become engaged to the beautiful socialite Caroline May, only to make front page news himself after a incident at her family's house on New Year's Day 1877. Bennett turned up for the party already 'one over the eight', and disgraced himself by urinating in the fireplace in full view of his intended, and her family.

Caroline's irate brother challenged Bennett Jnr to a duel, which was staged the following morning. Both men missed their target, but the opprobrium heaped on Bennett Jnr was so intense, that he felt obliged to leave the country.

He went to Paris, where his grandparents had lived in the late 18th Century, and started an International edition of the Herald Tribune, running his New York paper by cable. By 1900 he was residing on the estate of Louis XIV, the "Sun King", at Versailles, and planning further extravagant gestures.

That year he had a yacht built called the *Lysistrata,* which among other eccentricities, contained a Turkish Bath with a resident masseur , and a specially padded apartment, in which a cow was tethered to provide Bennett with fresh milk on a daily basis.

Also in that year he sponsored the first Gordon Bennett motor race from Paris to Lyon, with a first prize of 10,000 francs. It was won in 1902 by an Englishman Selwyn Edge, and so was destined for England the following year.

But Rolls' speed limit of 12 mph was still in place, so it went instead to Ireland . It was raced on a figure of eight course, between Ballyshannon and Carlow, and drew enormous crowds. It was the prototype for today's world-wide mega-rich Grand Prix circuit.

In 1906, the first Balloon race for the Gordon Bennett cup was held, and is still in existence today. It was won for Britain for the first time in 2008 when David Hemplemann-Adams triumphed in Albuquerque in New Mexico.

Then in 1909 Gordon Bennett took his Grand Prix concept into the skies, when he sponsored the first air race under his name at Rheims. The following year it was held in New York, and in 1911 this carnival arrived in the Isle of Sheppey.

There were originally 20 entrants for the Gordon Bennett Cup at Eastchurch on July 1st, but technical problems with some aircraft, and prior engagements for some pilots, whittled the number down to six. By the time the race began there were only five, because one of them had crashed while performing a demonstration lap of the course.

Over 10,000 aviation enthusiasts flooded on to the island to watch the race. Automobiles clogged the narrow lanes, and the Sheppey Light Railway could not cope with the influx of passengers, despite running 15 special trains , two of them from London. At one stage, there were 1,000 ticket holders waiting for a train at the tiny Sheerness East station. Faced with a two-hour wait for transportation, many of them began walking along the railway line in the direction of Eastchurch.

Confronted with such mass defiance of railway regulations, an angry stationmaster ordered his staff to take the names and addresses of the impatient travellers, declaring that he intended to have them prosecuted for trespassing on railway property.

Public entry fees for the race were 5 shillings per person, and for car and driver it was ten shillings. More than 200 cars were in the parking area when the race began, with members of the Royal Aero Club having their special enclosure sited in the most advantageous position. There was even a roped square on the crest of Standford Hill for the use of the Press.

The contest was won by American Charles Weyman, who completed the 25 laps of the six kilometre circuit in one hour, eleven minutes and 36 seconds, at an average speed of 78.11 mph.

The GB Cup continued until 1920 when it was superseded by the King's Cup, and the Schneider Trophy races for seaplanes.

In 1914 at the age of 73, Gordon Bennett married the widowed daughter of Paul Reuter, the founder of the international news agency. He died in France in 1918, but the French have certainly not forgotten him. Those of you who have visited the French Open Tennis championships at Stade Roland Garros, named after another renowned aviator, will know that it is situated in the Avenue Gordon Bennett.

Perhaps the saddest memorial to this truly larger than life newspaper mogul, was the USS James Gordon Bennett, a sister ship to the munitions vessel USS Richard Montgomery which still lies off the Isle of Sheppey. The former was part of a convoy making the return journey from England to the USA in September 1943, but was among ten ships that were lost to enemy action.

John Brabazon and Icarus II

Samuel Cody

Brabazon Stone

Rolls take off at Shell Beach

Frank McClean-Tower Bridge August 1912

Rolls (behind wheel) and Wright Bros

Short Bros (Oswald, Horace, and Eustace)

Muswell plaque

Founding Fathers visit Muswell Manor May 1909
Standing Left to Right:
James Andrews (owner), Oswald, Horace and Eustace Short, Francis McClean, Griffith Brewer, Frank Hedges Butler, Dr. Lockyer, Warwick Wright
Sitting Left to Right:
JTC Moore-Brabazon, Wilbur and Orville Wright, Charles Rolls

Chapter 11
SOLDIERS, SAILORS AND AIRMEN

The Naval Dockyard at Sheerness had been envisaged as an extension to the already well-established construction and repair facilities at Chatham, where Nelson's flagship " Victory " had been built and launched in 1765.

It had taken almost 200 years for Pepys' original plans to be fulfilled and the installation to become fully operational. The first dry dock was built in 1708 , but extension and improvements had to be abandoned in the 1760's because of the generally poor sanitation, and an outbreak of malaria.

The Medway is a tidal river, with a particularly strong race in the lower reaches off Sheerness, and hulks of old ships had to be stationed to break the inflow, and stop erosion of the foreshore. These hulks were also used as accommodation for the workforce , but conditions were primitive , and it was extremely difficult to attract enough men.

Eventually convicts were housed in the hulks, and put to work as labourers after a serious fire in the 1820's destroyed much of what had been constructed. Then an outbreak of cholera in 1834 caused further suspension of activities. It was not until the arrival of mains water in the early 1860's, together with the railway which ran right into the Dockyard area , that the obstacles were overcome.

Both Chatham and Sheerness were run by the Royal Navy, and when the Royal Naval Air Service came into being at Eastchurch, and Lt Samson made the first seaplane flight from a warship off Sheerness in 1912 ,the island's military significance began to grow rapidly.

The Army and the Royal Artillery soon arrived to defend the coastline and installations , and by the start of the First World War, Sheppey had become a restricted military zone. There were training camps and units dotted all over the place. One such detachment, housed at the historic Shurland Hall near Eastchurch, did irreparable damage to the building.

When Sheppey's residents were issued with a "passport", which had to be shown on exit or entry, it became known as "Barbed Wire Island".

Flights of Inspiration

Short's operations at Eastchurch, and its status as a base for the defence of naval installations, saw several important developments in air and naval warfare. In 1914 it was taken over by the Government under the Defence of the Realm act, and became the Number One centre for Naval flying.

The first bomb-dropping experiments were done there, as well as the early developments in machine guns fired from a plane in flight. Air-to-ground wireless communication was also tested and developed, while a Lieutenant Briggs established a new British altitude record by soaring to 14,920 feet over Sheppey.

In 1916 a Gunnery School was established , although this was split into Air and Ground sections two years later, the Air section moving to Leysdown. When Shorts moved to Rochester they sold their workshops and hangars to the RNAS, and then all civilian activity came to an end in 1920, when the Air Ministry bought out the Royal Aero Club's total interests at Eastchurch for the sum of £13,620.

Eastchurch became home to the RAF's Armament and Gunnery School in 1922. Thereafter the number of Service personnel decreased, and the island suffered high unemployment and hardship during the next decade.

The 1939-45 conflict saw the return of both the passport and the "barbed wire " nickname , as Servicemen again poured into Sheppey. Very soon the airfield at Eastchurch,

Michael D. Britten

and the Dockyard at Sheerness were thrust into the front line,

Chapter 12
LIGHTS OUT

A quarter of a century had elapsed since John Brabazon's first flight when Charlie Arnold took over the Rose and Crown.

Mussel Manor had reverted to being an isolated house on windswept open farmland, sheds and hangars had disappeared from Shell Beach, and a casual visitor would not have been aware that anything untoward had occurred on the marshes at the eastern end of the island.

Leysdown looked, and was, a sleepy rural village to which mains electricity had not yet arrived. The only power came from a 110 volt privately- owned generator, from which cables ran to a few houses, including the Rose and Crown. It was sufficient to provide lighting, but nothing else, When Charlie hung a string of coloured light bulbs across the front of the pub to make it more attractive, he was curtly informed he was taking too much electricity, and threatened with being cut off, if he did not immediately remove them.

Most people were still using oil lamps, while heating depended on coal and wood fires. The Rose and Crown had fireplaces in both the Public and Saloon bars, another in the downstairs lounge, and two more in the two double bedrooms on the first floor. The other four single rooms in the third floor attic were unheated.

The pub's trade in those early days of Charlie's tenancy was erratic. There were less than 200 residents in Leysdown and the nearby Warden Bay area, and the houses and bungalows were well scattered. There was a passing trade of sorts, but Leysdown had few facilities, and even fewer visitors in the winter months. Not until the summer camping season, from June through to September, was there any noticeable improvement. It was a long way from being a business on which a family could thrive.

Dennis and Eileen went to school in Queenborough, travelling to and from Leysdown station, the terminus for the Sheppey Light Railway. That was a lot easier than trying to get to Sheerness via a bus route that only occasionally operated to Leysdown. Both left school at 14, Dennis to help his father around the pub, and Eileen to assist her far from strong mother with the household chores, and care for her baby brother John, who arrived in May 1935.

Charlie's chief assets were his experience of dealing with the public, which he had gained while running his two shops in London, and a healthy ration of commonsense. Nevertheless progress was slow, until the outbreak of World War Two in 1939 provided an unexpected fillip.

Although there were two hostelries in the centre of Eastchurch, the Crooked Billet and the Castle, Leysdown's Rose and Crown, four miles further east, quickly became the favourite "watering hole" for the pilots stationed at the aerodrome, and further a-field. New squadrons were continually arriving at Eastchurch for training and patrol work in the early period of hostilities, which became known as 'the phoney war', and flyers of all nationalities pitched up at the Rose and Crown, particularly at weekends.

Charlie had signalled that he would not be beholden to anyone by purchasing his own 110 volt generator, and installing it in the pub's garage.

It was a great unwieldy apparatus, with a huge flywheel, and a smelly paraffin engine, which charged a bank of 50 batteries. Yet it was enough to light the pub from top to bottom, and power as many coloured bulbs as he wanted.

Dennis was given the task of looking after this temperamental beast, having already started going to night school at the Technical College in Sheerness to study electrical engineering.

Charlie, mindful of the strict segregation of his own Service days, reacted to the influx of thirsty flyers by designating the Saloon bar as an 'officers only' zone. All other ranks were served in the Public bar, which led to an uneasy relationship between father and daughter.

Eileen was by then a pretty 16 year old, and it was not long before she fell in love with a pilot who flew Blenheims out of Detling, a fighter station just off the road between Sittingbourne and Maidstone. Charlie did not approve, and did what he could to prevent the romance flourishing, firstly by assigning his daughter to work in the Saloon which had become the unofficial "officers' mess".

Eileen responded by getting engaged to Sergeant Pilot Dick Bates, and spending most of her time in the Public bar, whenever he called at the Rose and Crown during the Spring of 1940.

That was when mains electricity, in the form of a 6,000 volt high tension cable, first arrived in Leysdown, to power facilities at the RAF establishment between the village and Muswell Manor.

Flights of Inspiration

The Detling and Eastchurch squadrons were heavily engaged in Channel patrols, and increasingly in combat with the Luftwaffe as the German armed forces swept remorselessly westward through the Low Countries and into France. Sergeant Bates and the rest of the Blenheim pilots were in the thick of the action throughout April and May.

One day in early June Dick Bates did not turn up for a date with Eileen. He had been shot down over the beaches at Dunkirk.

As was the custom with RAF pilots at that time, he had written a last letter to his sweetheart, and she was heartbroken when it was delivered after his death was confirmed. She never showed it to anyone, not even her mother, or twin brother.

Like Eileen, Dennis never forgot Dick Bates. Many years later he penned a tribute to the brave English pilot in an effort to get his own children to understand their aunt's heartache , and the poignancy of those desperate times.

It read: "Many years ago I sat in the bar of a pub in Leysdown, talking to a young man. He was a Sergeant Pilot stationed at Detling near Maidstone. A quiet, easy to talk to bloke. We spoke just of ordinary things, the weather, would it rain tomorrow, what was on at the local cinema.

"He was waiting for a girl he was engaged to. When she arrived and they prepared to leave, we shook hands and said "good night, probably see you tomorrow", and off they went.

"The next morning he took off in his Blenheim aircraft, and flew to Dunkirk in France. And he was no more."

Chapter 13
EVACUATION

Shortly before I was born, my grandparents had bought a small bungalow at Minster in preparation for Percy's retirement from the Metropolitan Police. He was on the verge of completing 25 years service, most of it in the City of London division, and was almost 50.

Just before the two landmarks were reached, he was found to have contracted tuberculosis. It was hoped that a move to the seaside would prove beneficial, and in the summer of 1938 they took up residence at 39 Queens Road ,close to Minster Abbey. They re-named the bungalow "Kandalah" after the hill station where they had met in India.

My mother and father were able to visit them, and take me along too, but this happy family scenario was soon shattered by preparations for World War Two. The British Army was at that time a small professional force, and conscription would be inevitable in the event of a full-scale conflict. With war clouds gathering, the Government stepped up preparations by appealing for volunteers in various trades. The Army was particularly short of qualified driver-mechanics.

My father, along with most of the lorry drivers at his company, decided to answer the call, reasoning that it would be better to volunteer than await call up. My mother disagreed, feeling that his first duty was to his family.

Much later my Gran told me there had been a series of bitter arguments, and many tears, but my father would not be dissuaded, and not long after my second birthday he was among the advance elements of the British Expeditionary Force sent to France. Before he departed, it was arranged that my mother and I would move in with Gran and Grand-dad Clarke at Minster.

The bungalow was not very large, consisting of two bedrooms, a small bathroom, lounge and kitchen, but it had a long, narrow garden with apple and pear trees, fruit bushes, and a sizeable vegetable patch. It backed on to the grounds of a large vicarage, which was home to the local clerics.

On its right hand side was a fenced field, roughly 100 yards square, bordered by a Co-operative Society grocery store. This field was later to be home to an enormous, grey barrage balloon, which I called "the elephant in the sky".

To what extent an adult can remember childhood events has always been a subject for conjecture. But I can clearly recall being re-introduced to my father when he was given leave after being evacuated from Dunkirk. My mother and grandmother had gone down to Dover on the train in the hope that he would be among the BEF survivors.

He wasn't there, and it was suggested they try Ramsgate. They found him huddled in a blanket in a church hall, recovering from the experience of crossing a choppy English Channel in an over-loaded motor cruiser, one of the hundreds of small boats that had gone across to snatch the troops off the beaches.

I also vividly remember the 'writing in the sky' above that part of Kent, which must have been the vapour trails created by the RAF and Luftwaffe pilots in the Battle of Britain. Both events took place in 1940, when I was three years old.

My grandfather used to sit me on his knee and tell me stories about lions and tigers before I was put to bed, and I also remember crying when I was told he had gone away. In fact his health had deteriorated so much that he had been taken into Barming Heath Hospital near Maidstone. He died of pulmonary tuberculosis in April 1942 and was buried in the cemetery there. He was only 56.

Chapter 14
UNCLES

Grand-dad Percy's death deeply affected my mother and grandmother, both emotionally and economically. It meant they had to fend for themselves: money was tight, strict rationing was in force, and I had just started at a private school, where fees had to be paid.

At four years and four months, I was the youngest pupil at the Santa Maria Catholic School, on the corner of King's road leading to Minster beach, no more than 100 yards from "Kandalah". It was run by two sisters called Harriet and Winifred, and there were only 30 or so children up to the age of 10. The girls outnumbered the boys by a ratio of four to one.

We would all assemble at 9.00 am each morning to say our prayers, and then split into two groups for classes. On the opposite side of the road was a small field, where the girls played rounders and the boys kicked around a football.

In addition to basic Arithmetic and English, and learning to write, Music was also on the syllabus. I was set to practise endless scales, one-handed on a piano, whose keyboard I could reach only by piling three cushions onto its stool. By the age of five I could play a tune , but only one tune ,"The Bluebells of Scotland" .

I was supposed to read the notes from the sheet music placed in front of me. In reality I memorised the keys which my tiny fingers should depress. I never understood the bewildering array of black and white symbols and other squiggly bits, so I could never play any other tune.

But that didn't stop the two sisters plonking me on the stool whenever my mother or other visitors came to the school, and ordering me to play my party piece, as an example of their teaching skills.

To pay for all this learning my mother got a job in the local council offices, using her shorthand -typing skills to good effect, and becoming secretary to the Borough Surveyor. His name was Ted Brading, and he soon became known to me as "Uncle Ted". He was a small man with a round face, friendly smiling eyes, and a neat moustache. He also smoked a pipe, and had a car in which he used to let me sit, and play with the wheel.

He began calling at our Queens Road bungalow at weekends. He would bring a present, usually some item of food, for my grandmother, and there was always a small bag of sweets for me, either dolly mixtures, or a packet of sweet cigarettes, the sugary substitutes for the real thing.

Then one weekend he didn't arrive. Deprived of my customary sweets, I asked where Uncle Ted was, but no answer was forthcoming, and he gradually faded from memory, much as my father, who by then was part of the Eighth Army fighting Rommel's Afrika Korps.

It was back to routine, with meals of spam or corned beef and potatoes or greens, grown in our vegetable patch. For dessert it was usually gelatine, a sort of cross between yoghurt and sour milk, which I detested, or tapioca with a dollop of jam. At weekends my Gran would take the ration books to the next door Co-Op, and return with a small joint of lamb or beef which she would cook for Sunday lunch.

The bits left over would be minced and re-cycled as a shepherd's pie in midweek, or put into a big pot which always seemed to be simmering on the stove. There was the occasional apple or pear, but once Uncle Ted stopped coming, sweet treats were few and far between.

Then one day I cycled home from school on my little three-wheeler, and toddled into a furious argument between Mum and Gran. My usual tea of bread and jam

Flights of Inspiration

sandwich was not on the table, because they were shouting and throwing plates at each other .

Naturally I had no idea what it was all about, and I was sent to my room and told not to come out until called. Eventually the rumpus ended ,and by then starving hungry, I was allowed to emerge.

Whether it was the following weekend ,or some time later ,1 cannot recall, but a new 'uncle' began calling at the house to take Mum out. This one didn't bring sweets, instead he brought bags of Smith's Crisps, the salt and vinegar version, with the salt wrapped in a little blue bag inside the cellophane cover.

He placed them in our gooseberry bush, and I was sent down the garden to retrieve them. For years I thought that crisps grew there alongside the fruit !

He was a bit taller than Uncle Ted, and also older, and sometimes I went with him and Mum to the pictures.

Eventually she told me his name was Uncle Charlie, and that he lived in a house called the Rose and Crown at Leysdown. What I didn't know was that he was to have a major influence on the rest of my life.

Chapter 15
SLEEPING QUARTERS

The plate-throwing episode between my mother and grandmother proved to be the prelude to a series of events that resulted in me having the choice of four beds in which to sleep .

One of them was not really a bed, rather a drop-sided cot in a hole in the ground underneath the apple trees at Kandalah in Queen's Road, Minster. It was the Andersen shelter which Grand-dad Percy had helped to build in the latter months of 1939, when the hole was dug by workmen with shovels, then lined and roofed with corrugated iron.

Grand-dad then piled the earth that had been excavated on top of the roof, and replaced the turf. There was a flight of steps down to a metal door and behind it were two metal beds and my cot in between. It was dark, damp, and cold down there, the only lighting being from a couple of candles, and a grill in the door. There was no heating.

Flights of Inspiration

Whenever the air- raid siren sounded Mum or Gran would collect me from my bedroom and we would all go down to the shelter. Sometimes we were there for most of the night. At other times it would be only for an hour or so.

On one occasion the Andersen probably saved our lives. German aircraft were in the habit of using Sheppey as a dumping ground for the bombs they had been prevented from dropping at their primary targets, like the Short's seaplane works at Rochester, or the Chatham and Sheerness Dockyards. All three were protected by anti-aircraft defences on either side of the Medway.

One night, after the ' elephant in the sky' had been sent aloft from the field next door to join the other barrage balloons flying over the island, a discarded bomb demolished the Cooperative store where Gran shopped, and a stick of incendiaries landed in the vicinity of my school just across the road.

The noise was deafening and the ground shook violently. We stayed in the shelter all night because Mum and Gran were too scared to come out, in case there were more planes around.

There wasn't, but several of our windows were shattered and slates had come off the roof because of the blast from the bomb that hit the Co-op store. That was the last time

I went down the shelter, for very soon afterwards I found I had two more new homes.

The first was at No 2 Noreen Avenue, just off the road from Sheerness, and nearer to where Mum worked at the Council Offices. I later discovered it had been bought for her by Charlie Arnold, who had been the reason why she and Gran had been throwing plates at each other. It had stairs, and I had a big room all to myself at the back of the house ,overlooking the rear garden .

The other was the Rose and Crown at Leysdown where Mum went to stay at weekends. I had one of the four bedrooms in the attic, that had once been occupied by Short's workers at the Shellbeach Airfield next to Muswell Manor.

From Monday to Friday while I was at school, I stayed with my Gran in Queen's Road , or with Mum at Noreen Avenue. During the school holidays I would be at Leysdown. These arrangements began in 1943 but were soon altered again, for Mum gave up her job at the Council Offices early in 1944, and went to live permanently at the Rose and Crown.

In her letters to my father she told him that she had a new job helping to run a public house , a condition being that she lived in, and of the arrangements involving my schooling. As the Eighth Army invasion of Sicily was imminent ,and he had no immediate prospect of leave, it was a situation he had to accept.

All this I gleaned long after the conflict was over. Until some six months after my eighth birthday I was a very confused little boy.

Chapter 16
UNDER FIRE

As soon as he was 18 Dennis applied to join the RAF and train as a pilot. When he was told he would have to wait for another two years, he put the long hours at night school to good use by getting a job as an electrician's mate at the Sheerness Electric Light Company. This body was responsible for maintenance of the power supply throughout Sheppey, and Dennis was given a bicycle to get about the island.

Meanwhile his parents were counting their blessings after a devastating German raid on Eastchurch aerodrome which initially put it out of action, then forced its closure as a frontline operational station. The raid came on August 13th 1940 when the Luftwaffe switched their attention to RAF airfields, rather than Central London.

Eastchurch, which had become home to 1300 Polish airmen who had escaped their country's invasion by

Flights of Inspiration

Germany the previous year, and was a hive of activity, was one of the first to be hit. A force of 50 bombers got through the RAF fighter defences and caused havoc. There were many casualties, and great damage to installations. In addition all six Spitfires of 266 squadron , and five Blenheims were destroyed, having failed to get off the ground. The runways were left badly cratered.

Although planes were able to land and take off very soon afterwards, further attacks during August convinced the Air Ministry that Eastchurch was too vulnerable, and its squadrons were dispersed to other airfields like Detling, Manston, and Gravesend. Thereafter Eastchurch was mainly used for training, its airfield reserved for emergency use only.

Leysdown also received its first and only attack of the war at this time. A German plane flew at low level from east to west, dropping 16 bombs along the road leading to Eastchurch. Some fell on the former airfield and one demolished Tomlin's store on the corner of Station Road opposite the Rose and Crown. Another landed in Leysdown Road severing the new mains electricity cable. The rest fell either in gardens or on open ground. No one was hurt.

Dennis recalled that he had been in the bathroom with Eileen when they heard the plane approaching. "As we looked out of the window Eileen said " that one is very low," and I said "crikey its got German markings on it." Then there were a lot of loud bangs. "

Eileen had taken a long time to get over the death of Dick Bates , but found , as so many did, that time was a great healer, and she had become attracted to a Canadian airman attached to a radar unit on the cliffs at Warden Point. She and Bob Tanton were married at St Clement's Church at Leysdown and produced their first son John, before Eileen left Sheppey and returned with Bob to his home town of Penticton in British Columbia at the end of WW2. They had two further children, Barbara, and Stevie.

Tragedy again struck the Arnold family in 1941 when Charlie's wife Emma died of heart trouble at the age of 49. She had produced six children, but only three of them reached maturity.

Dennis spent three years with the local electricity company before he was accepted by the RAF. He did his early flying training at Carlisle where he went solo after 12 hours on Tiger Moths, and was given special leave to attend his sister's wedding, before being shipped out to South Africa.

By mid-1944 the RAF were not losing as many fighter pilots as they had anticipated, and Dennis was kept languishing in Pretoria and Johannesburg for almost six months before he was sent up to Gwelo in Southern

Flights of Inspiration

Rhodesia, now Zimbabwe, to continue flying training. Anthony Wedgewood Benn, who later renounced his peerage to become Labour politician Tony Benn, was on one of the courses ahead of him. Dennis trained on Harvards and had just gained his wings to become a fully fledged Sergeant Pilot, when the Commanding Officer told him the war in Europe was over. Back home there had been events of which he was totally unaware.

Chapter 17
SHORT SHRIFT FOR SHORTS

The Shorts move to Rochester in 1917 coincided with the death of Horace, their chief engineer and technical inspiration, at the relatively young age of 45.

He had suffered from hydrocephaly since contracting meningitis in childhood, which resulted in his head being two and a half times normal size. Yet the condition did nothing to impair an amazing intellect. So knowledgeabe was he on so many subjects, that it was said he also had a brain two and half times normal size.

Horace had enjoyed an adventurous life. As a young man he had left Britain for Australia, but on the way had been shipwrecked, and ended up on a Pacific island inhabited by cannibals. His unusual appearance and ability to shoot wild animals with a gun he had salvaged, convinced them he was a god.

Flights of Inspiration

He was able to escape, and before long was running a silver mine in Mexico at the age of 23. Horace had enough capital at that time to be able to send Eustace the not inconsiderable sum of £500 to tide the family over , following the death of their father. Eustace used most of it to finance his balloon workshop in Battersea.

Horace was working on the development of steam turbines when his younger siblings suggested forming the Short Brothers company to manufacture aircraft. He immediately showed his versatility by producing blueprints of the Wright Flyer they had been licensed to build, after going to Paris to inspect and measure the machine. He then masterminded their construction at Shell Beach where he was always the first to be summoned when repairs were required.

He oversaw the completion of the contract to build six Wright Flyers, and then put his innovatory skills to good effect when the company moved to Eastchurch.

Horace was responsible for the first Shorts seaplane in 1912 which Lieutenant Samson flew from HMS Africa and HMS Hibernia, the introduction of floats and folding wings, and the production of the S184 which became the mainstay of the fledgling RNAS. This plane was the first to use a torpedo to sink a ship, accounting for a Turkish freighter during the Gallipoli campaign in 1915.

After his death, youngest brother Oswald took over as chief designer and within a year had introduced aluminium alloys into airplane construction, a development that was years ahead of its time. Whereas other manufacturers, like the German Junkers company were experimenting with a corrugated type of all-metal fuselage, Oswald concentrated on the smooth stressed-skin version.

It had its first expression in the sleek Silver Streak which first flew in 1920, although it was not generally recognised as being the plane of the future. Oswald persisted in his belief, and succeeded brilliantly with the Singapore seaplane of 1926, which had an all-metal hull. It had a wing span of 93 feet, was capable of 130 mph, and was used by Sir Alan Cobham on his survey flight round the African Continent the following year.

It was followed by the more powerful Calcutta which became the civil flying boat used by Imperial Airways, and led eventually to the Sunderland, the mainstay of Coastal Command's anti-submarine campaign during World War Two.

While Oswald concentrated on design , Eustace became chairman of Shorts, and also a keen aviator in his early fifties, as detailed in the separate chapter entitled Cockles and Mussels. Sadly he suffered a heart attack while landing a seaplane on the River Medway near the

Rochester works in 1932. Along with Horace he is buried in Hampstead Cemetery in north London.

Oswald replaced him as Chairman of the company, until it was nationalised at the end of 1942. He resigned at that point, but remained Honorary Life President until his death in 1969 at the age of 86.

One of the enduring mysteries of British aviation is why none of the Shorts Brothers was honoured by the nation for their outstanding contribution to aircraft development, in particular seaplane and flying boat design.

There were 'gongs' a-plenty for the aviators, but nothing for these pioneers of construction, not during their lifetime, or retrospectively. Could it be that Oswald's rejection of a personal MBE in 1919 led to all of them being blacklisted?

Oswald expressed the opinion that the award "did not reflect the contribution the three brothers had made to aviation". He was right.

Chapter 18
THE STRANGER

Dennis Arnold was still wending his way home from Cape Town when, in the summer of 1945, a stranger came to the side entrance of the Rose and Crown one Saturday morning. He looked at me kicking a battered old football against a wall, then rang the bell on the door of the little porch.

A few minutes later 'Uncle' Charlie called me to come inside and get changed into my school clothes, then go upstairs to see my mother. Although it was almost midday, she was still in bed, suffering from a heavy cold and sore throat. There were tears on her cheeks as she told me I would be going away, and that I had to be a good boy. She gave me a hug and a small purse with some coins in it, then I was sent downstairs.

The stranger took me out to a car parked on the forecourt and sat me in the back seat. In no time at all we were in

Flights of Inspiration

Sheerness and preparing to board a train. I had never been on one, and I was thrilled by the sight of the steam engine and the green carriages waiting at the platform. Not much was said until I asked where we were going.

"We are going to another Granny and Grand-dad in Bournemouth " replied the stranger, who then began to explain that he was my father, and that I would be living with him, and not my mother from then on.

This situation had arisen as a direct result of the divorce proceedings my father had initiated when he discovered the true nature of my mother's relationship with Charlie Arnold. The court had ruled that my mother was the guilty party, and that custody and upbringing of the child of the broken marriage should be undertaken by the innocent party, my father, even though I did not remember him. The best interests of the child were not paramount in those days.

It was almost dark when I arrived at another new home after the train journey to London, then another longer one from Waterloo to Bournemouth Central, There were two further bus trips before father and son were walking through the front door of No 2 Oxford Lane in the village of Kinson on the Hampshire-Dorset borders. This was to be my home for the next three years, and not one I remember with any affection.

It was a very cramped two-bedroom ground floor maisonette , in a block of eight, which my father's parents Charles and Annie had purchased in the 1930's with the compensation they had received when their small farm near Grantham had been split in two by the new A1 trunk road.

They augmented their meagre pension by letting out their spare bedroom for short periods to young boys from the local Dr Barnardo's home. None of them were there for longer than a month. This arrangement continued despite my arrival on a permanent basis, so for most of my time at Kinson, I shared my bedroom with a succession of pre-teenagers whose names I have long forgotten.

Annie was a fearsome looking woman in her seventies, with a hooked nose and bushy eyebrows. Charles was considerably older, had a permanent limp, and always used a walking stick, even when tending a large rear garden that was given over almost entirely to vegetables.

I was enrolled at Kinson County Primary School, only 150 yards away at the other end of Oxford Lane, which was a young boys' paradise. There was a muddy stream, blackberry bushes and a long straight stretch which was our football and cricket pitch . At that time there were very few cars, so most of my time outside of school was spent playing games and scrapping in the lane with other kids, using telegraph poles for wickets, and our coats for goal posts.

We did that every weekday until 6.45 pm , at which point everyone rushed indoors to listen to the latest episode of Dick Barton Special Agent on BBC radio. Then it was tea and bedtime.

On Saturdays I was put to running shopping errands, while Sundays were given over to religion. In the morning Gran took me to church until she felt I was old enough to walk the mile and a half to St Andrew's C of E on my own. In the afternoon it was Sunday School in an old house on the village green, then if it wasn't raining it was back to the village church for Evensong. By the time I was ten I could tell what hymns the congregation would be singing solely by the numbers posted above the pulpit !

My father put in few appearances. As soon as he had delivered me he returned to London where he was trying to make a living selling vegetables door-to-door. He had bought a second-hand lorry in which he used to travel to Brentford Market at 5.00 am each morning to buy produce, and then tour smart residential areas south of the River Thames, like Worcester Park, Cheam, and Ewell. Gradually he built up a clientele of housewives and widows eager to buy fresh fruit and salad ingredients at a cheaper price than in the shops.

Just after my 11th birthday in 1948 I took the eleven-plus examination ,and passed to earn a place in the first form at Bournemouth Grammar School for Boys in Castle Lane. The news was relayed to my father ,who came down from London, and I was taken into the town centre to be fitted out with a completely new set of clothes and shoes, including the requisite blazer, cap, and tie.

My days as a street urchin were over. The other kids in Oxford Lane thought I had gone "posh".

Chapter 19
OVER THE POND

In the first ten years of aviation virtually every significant development in Europe was of a military nature. Apart from a few early sorties in France when passengers went aloft for short flights, civil aviation had taken second place to the demands of the Great War.

Interest was not rekindled until a few days after the Armistice in 1918 when newspaper magnate Lord Northcliffe, publisher of the Daily Mail, resurrected the offer he had first made in 1913 of a £10,000 prize for the first Transatlantic flight.

The only stipulations were that the starting point had to be either in the USA, Canada, or Newfoundland, or the British Isles, and that the journey had to be non-stop and completed within 72 hours. This challenge was the spur for two Britons to make one of the most inspirational flights in history, and open the door to long distance civilian travel.

Because the chances of overcoming the perils of this dangerous venture would be considerably improved by flying west to east, thus taking advantage of the prevailing Atlantic winds, contestants flocked to Newfoundland in the Spring of 1919.

Among them were the Australian Harry Hawker who was later to team so successfully with Tommy Sopwith at Hawker Siddeley, and another civilian flyer Ken MacKenzie-Grieve. There were two or three other British pairs preparing their aircraft for the challenge by the time two RAF airmen, Captain John Alcock and Lieutenant Arthur Whitten-Brown arrived at St Johns, on May 13. They had sailed across the Atlantic on the liner *Mauretania,* but their aircraft had been crated and transported by a freighter that was not due for another two weeks.

Alcock was an aviation pioneer, having gained his pilot's certificate at the age of 20 and become an instructor in acrobatics. He had won a DSC for his exploits with the RFC during the Gallipoli campaign.

Whitten-Brown's parents were American, but he was born in Scotland, and had volunteered for the British Army in which he fought on the Western Front before transferring to the Royal Flying Corps as an observer.

Flights of Inspiration

He was an expert on astral navigation. Their aircraft was a converted Vickers Vimy bomber, fitted with two 350 horse power Rolls Royce engines. Its cruising speed was 90 mph, and it had a range of 2,400 miles.

While Alcock and Brown were still waiting for their craft to arrive and hunting for a flat field suitable for take off, Hawker and Mackenzie-Grieve took off on May 18th in their Sopwith biplane, determined to be the first to cross "the pond". They were well past the point of no return, when their oil pressure began to drop rapidly and the engines started to splutter. They were also being blown off course by a strong northerly wind.

Fearing the worst they began to circle, desperately looking for a vessel. After nearly two hours of fruitless search, and dropping ever closer to the ocean, they spotted one and put down in the sea ahead. They were given up for lost, until a week later when news came through that a Danish freighter had rescued them. Hawker and Mackenzie-Grieve were given a heroes' welcome when they eventually arrived at the Aero Club headquarters in London.

The Americans were also hell-bent on making the Atlantic crossing, but their attention was centred on the Azores, not the British Isles. Their outstanding designer Glenn Curtiss, who had sold many of his seaplanes to Britain during the war, had recently supplied the US Navy with his latest Flying Boat. They planned to send three of them, "guarded" all the way by a flotilla of American warships, in case of accidents.

All three took off on May 16, but only the third, captained by a Lt-Commander Albert Read reached its destination unaided. The first came down 200 miles short of the islands, as did the second after losing its way in fog. Both crews were rescued. Read's plane completed the near 1400 mile flight in 15 hours, then later flew to mainland Portugal, and from there to England. However that still left the Daily Mail prize unclaimed, and it remained so after Hawker's attempt ended in near disaster.

By Saturday June 14 Alcock and Brown were ready, and arrived early in the morning to begin the task of filling their plane with 870 gallons of gasoline, and 40 gallons of oil. For food they took sandwiches and chocolate, and for drink they had a flask of coffee and some bottles of brandy and beer.

A strong westerly cross wind was blowing and they waited several hours for it to abate, until shortly after one pm local time Alcock decided he could get the Vickers Vimy airborne without crashing. Even so, it was a close run thing as the lumbering plane just cleared a line of trees on the hills ahead and slowly climbed out to sea.

Eighteen years earlier the first wireless signal sent across the Atlantic had been received at the Marconi station in the capital St John's. That same base sent the news of their take off to every ship in the North Atlantic, asking them to signal the plane's position if sighted, or give assistance if necessary.

As they reached cruising height of 3,000 feet, gathering speed because of the strong tailwind, Brown began testing their wireless by sending a message back to St John's. He had barely started when the generator suddenly ceased to function. Its energy came from a small wind-driven propeller underneath the fuselage that could not be seen from the cockpit. So Brown climbed out onto the lower wing to investigate as Alcock tried to keep the craft, by then travelling over 100 mph, on an even keel.

Three of the propeller blades had snapped during take off, and Brown knew their wireless was useless. They could not send or receive messages, and neither could they get their bearings from any ship they passed. They were totally on their own.

As if that was not bad enough, they encountered further problems as dusk fell. Their starboard engine began spluttering and coughing because of damage to the exhaust, then they ran into a thick fog bank, rendering Brown's astral navigation impossible. Alcock had to take the plane up to 12,000 feet before the stars became visible.

They sustained themselves throughout the long night hours with sandwiches and brandy until just as dawn was breaking they hurtled into another dense fog bank and soon became completely disorientated. The instrument panel showed they were not flying on an even keel, and that they were rapidly losing height.

The plane was still in thick cloud at 500 feet, and it was not until they were a mere 100 feet above the ocean that they emerged into the clear. Only Alcock's split second realisation that the plane was almost upside down, and his skill in righting it, saved them from disaster. They levelled out, the right way up, just 50 feet above the waves.

The perils were far from over. A few hours later they flew into a storm, firstly lashing rain, then snow and sleet. Alcock climbed to 9000 feet in an attempt to get above it, only to see the gasoline gauge mounted on one of the struts ahead of the cockpit, become completely obscured by ice. Worse still the rest of the plane began to ice up, and he had great difficulty in moving the controls. Then the air intakes became clogged with snow and ice and the engines began misfiring.

Brown once again left the cockpit, several times climbing on to the wings and clinging on to the struts as he scraped the ice away from the intakes. One slip in the freezing, howling wind and he would be gone. Alcock would not have survived either. Not a moment too soon they emerged from the clouds to see the outline of the coast of Ireland looming through the mist ahead.

Flights of Inspiration

They made landfall at Clifden in Galway, and decided to come down immediately rather than attempt to fly on to London. They circled the town and located the radio station where they noticed what seemed a large tract of level ground. They mistook the waving of men on the roof as gestures of welcome instead of warning, and touched down on the stretch of green sward.

After no more than 100 yards the Vickers Vimy nose-dived into the soggy soil. They had landed in a Connemara peat bog, shortly after 8.20 am.

When asked where they had come from, they proudly answered "America." Word of their arrival spread so rapidly, that next day the New York newspapers carried the front page story of their achievement. Alcock and Brown had flown the Atlantic covering 1980 miles in just over 16 hours.

It had been a triumph of courage over adversity and not only did they richly deserve Lord Northcliffe's prize and the public acclaim, but also the knighthoods that were immediately bestowed on them by King George V.

Chapter 20
ALL ABOARD

The first Transatlantic crossing by Alcock and Brown was soon followed by the first England to Australia flight, also in a converted Vickers bomber.

During November and December 1919 two Australian brothers Keith and Ross Smith flew from London to Darwin in 27 days to win a £10,000 prize presented by the Australian Government. The Golden Age of Aviation was about to begin.

One of the earliest examples of passenger flight had been in March 1911 after Frenchman Louis Breguet had built a biplane powered by a Renault engine. He took off from an airfield at Douai with eleven passengers and flew them three miles. Then the Russian Igor Sikorsky produced the world's first four engine aircraft, a biplane with a wing span of 101 feet. It had an enclosed heated cabin, and an open promenade deck at the rear of the fuselage where passengers could enjoy "fresh air".

In June 1914 it flew non-stop from St Petersburg to Kiev in the Ukraine, a distance of almost 1600 miles.

The Great War put an end to further developments in civilian flying, so much so that it was illegal in Britain until May 1919, principally to allow the Air Ministry to establish a Civil Aviation department, and for the Government to formulate air and traffic regulations.

Elsewhere there were no such embargoes, and the first steps towards establishing regular passenger services were taken in France and Germany, and also in the United States, where the early emphasis was on transporting mail, rather than human beings.

Even when the authorities lifted the ban on May 1, progress in Britain was slow, although the RAF had begun running a mail service to Paris from their aerodrome at Kenley, just south of Croydon. Among the Government ministers who made use of it while attending the post-war conferences which resulted in the Treaty of Versailles, was that noted aviation enthusiast Winston Churchill.

A company called Air Transport and Travel operated the first British commercial flight from Hounslow to Paris in July 1919. Its first passenger was a member of the Pilkington Glass Manufacturers who was charged £50 for the trip. A month later AT and T started the world's first daily scheduled international service between Hounslow and Le Bourget, using a De Havilland 4 converted bomber, powered by a Rolls Royce Eagle engine. It was able to carry two passengers in a covered rear cockpit at a speed of 120 mph.

In March 1920 the London terminal was moved from Hounslow to another former RAF airfield at Croydon, in open country south of the town.

Meanwhile Churchill, who became Air Minister shortly afterwards, became the driving force behind a Government-backed competition to produce the first custom-built passenger airliner, A prize of £7,500 was offered but attracted only three entrants, Vickers, Bristol, and Handley Page.

The winner was the latter's W8 aircraft based on an old bomber design, using two Rolls Royce engines. It could carry 12 passengers in an enclosed, comfortable cabin furnished with wicker chairs and tables, which also contained a toilet compartment.

By today's standards it was decidedly primitive and extremely noisy, and it was advisable to wear a flying suit, but aviation was then very much an adventure, although progress during the 1920's was so rapid that it swiftly became routine, if only for the well-to-do.

Flights of Inspiration

In 1921 it was possible to fly to Paris for £6 single and £12 return, which put the journey well beyond the reach of the general public for whom £1.50 was a good weekly wage.

Three British companies operated flights out of Croydon, running services to various European cities, but all were in financial difficulties at some stage, and owed much to Churchill's influence in securing Government subsidies to keep them operating.

It was not a situation that could continue indefinitely, and very soon the Government pressured them to merge. In April 1924 a new single company, Imperial Airways, was formed. Britain's national flag carrier began life with just 15 aircraft, operating from old RAF hangars and workshops, using a grass airfield ringed by ex-Army wooden huts that had been converted into offices, and a passenger reception area.

Heathrow, Gatwick and Stansted were a long way down the line !

Chapter 21
TOUCH DOWN

After spending the best part of two years in South Africa, Dennis was in no hurry to return to the rural tranquillity of Leysdown.

He was a newly-qualified pilot, but the Royal Air Force had thousands of trained aviators when the war ended, and only a small proportion would be retained for the slimmer peacetime service. So he switched from air to ground crew, and became an airfield controller, working at various RAF stations in East Anglia for 18 months. One of them was Graveley, just south of Huntingdon, which had been home to The Pathfinders during the war.

While there he was persuaded by a fellow sergeant to visit one of the many "olde worlde" country pubs in the area, the Cross Keys, in the village of Upwood. This 17th Century hostelry had oak beams, a roaring log fire, and also an attractive barmaid who was the daughter of the landlord.

Dennis met her again a few days later while shopping in Huntingdon, and so began the courtship which resulted in their marriage on the first day of March, 1947, six weeks after the RAF decided they no longer required his services.

Naturally the wedding reception was held at the Cross Keys, and after the honeymoon Dennis and Daphne headed for the Isle of Sheppey, with the intention of setting up home in a bungalow his father owned at Warden Point. It had also been used by twin sister Eileen and her husband Bob, before they left for Canada.

Dennis and Daphne began working at the Rose and Crown where Charlie Arnold was anticipating a busy summer holiday trade. This arrangement lasted only three months, before the newly-weds were heading back to Huntingdonshire, having quickly discovered, as I did later, that Charlie was an impossibly hard task-master, especially to family members.

Dennis found work as an electrician for the Air Ministry and for two years the newly-weds lived on a local airfield in what had formerly been officers' quarters.

There they might have stayed had it not been for an extraordinary accident which saw the death of his maternal grandfather Charles Moore, right outside the Rose and Crown. Emma's father had just taken his dog out for a walk when it pulled hard on its lead, and the old man lost his balance.

He tumbled under the wheels of a passing tractor driven by the son of a local farmer, who had no time to stop or avoid him. It was a tragic mishap for which no one was to blame.

Dennis returned to Leysdown for the funeral, and this time he and Daphne were given the welcome that had been missing two years previously. The rapprochement led to him firstly finding work as an electrician, then setting up business in a café that Charlie had constructed on land he had purchased in Wing Road.

Up till then our paths had not crossed. I knew of him, but had never met him. He was in South Africa when I first went to the Rose and Crown, and he did not return to Leysdown until after I had been taken to Bournemouth.

When we did meet early in 1950, it was after we had both decided that we preferred to keep our respective fathers at arm's length. Neither of them were able to converse with, or more importantly, listen to their offspring. They thought the way to solve difficulties was to impose their own will, or ignore them altogether.

In Charlie's case his martinet approach, coupled with his embarrassment in emotional situations, led to varying degrees of alienation with his sons. It was to result in considerable heartache in later years when daughter Carol's teenage exuberance coincided with the advent of the "swinging Sixties".

Chapter 22
REVERSE GEAR

I enjoyed being at Bournemouth Grammar. I was chosen for the School Under -13 football and cricket teams, although I was only a first-former, and I did well enough at lessons to win a place in the top 2A class for the second year. I also made plenty of new friends.

By now I was old enough to take the bus into Bournemouth town centre on my own and join them on the wide sandy beaches during the long summer holiday. There were Sunday School outings to Swanage and Studland Bay, and always I was playing or watching cricket in Pelhams Park at Kinson. Occasionally I went fishing with the local boys in the River Stour at Longham. or to Sandbanks and the harbour at Poole.

When September arrived I was eager to get back to school and start playing football again, dreaming of winning a place in the Bournemouth Schools Under-15 side. I had got used to sharing a bedroom with total strangers, and as long as I returned home before dark, winter or summer, my grandparents more or less left me to my own devices.

I got into occasional scrapes, as boys do, but apart from falling from a horse-chestnut tree and knocking out some milk teeth in the pursuit of conkers, the summer of '49 was largely uneventful, until my father dropped another bombshell.

The weekend before I was due to return to school he arrived from London with the news that he was about to get married again, and that I would be going back with him to a new home in Chessington,

On his greengrocery round in suburbia he had met a war widow called Olwen who had a nine year old daughter named Avril, The four of us would be a ready-made family, or so he thought. What he had not counted on was my rebellious streak, which suddenly came to the surface, and Olwen's Welsh chapel upbringing which led to some hilariously embarrassing moments.

For instance I was not allowed to hang out washing on the garden line if it contained any female undergarments. They were always carefully removed before I was permitted to undertake that chore, and dried separately. Then there was the episode at the National Gallery after

I came home from school with a note suggesting that my woeful knowledge of art might be improved by a visit to the building which housed the nation's treasures.

At the first sight of the naked bodies on display, Olwen declared the place to be "disgusting", dragged Avril outside, and forced me, and my father, to follow.

She was also extremely house-proud, and did not take kindly to a stepson who always had muddy shoes or football boots, trying to get into her immaculate three-bedroom semi-detached home at number 12 Chessington Close, just behind the Bonesgate public house on the Ewell to Tolworth road. Anything wet or dirty had to be removed before entry was permitted, then I had to wear a pair of fluffy slippers so that no scratches were made on her polished lino surrounds.

My new step-sister hardly said a word to me for months. She went to a private school and was not allowed to go out to play with the other girls in the Close. Avril seemed to spend most of her time dressing and undressing dolls, and filling in her large collection of colouring books.

Olwen made it clear she didn't like me very much, and I have to admit the feeling was mutual. It also soon became obvious that she didn't think all that much of my father either. She refused to call him by his proper name Herbert, or Bert, as he was usually known. Instead she christened him John.

Flights of Inspiration

Then she decided that the truck in which he made his rounds, and parked overnight outside the house , was "lowering the tone of the neighbourhood." Either it had to be hidden away , or it had to go. It duly went, and my father took up hairdressing, which he used to do in the Army, working in a shop in Surbiton near the Blue Lagoon swimming pool. Every fortnight, regular as clockwork, I was taken there to have my hair washed and trimmed.

Two weeks after the autumn term had started my transfer from Bournemouth was confirmed, and I became a second-former at Epsom Grammar School, to which I made the four mile journey by bicycle, rain or shine.

I gained a place in the School football team, and indulged in every after-school activity I could in order to avoid the increasingly awkward atmosphere chez Olwen. I even joined the School's Chess club because it kept me there until 6.00 pm on Thursday evenings.

Saturdays were taken up with football, but there was no escaping Sundays, which invariably became family outings in my father's nearly-new second-hand car. One of my chores was to help him wash and polish it every Sunday morning to the standard required by her ladyship, whose brothers and sisters all seemed to live in one area of north west London.

By midday everything, and everyone ,was washed and prepared for the journey round the South Circular to Edgware or Stanmore ,where we would arrive in good time for Sunday lunch. Afterwards while the men went into the garden to smoke their pipes, and the women chatted in the lounge, the children were sent upstairs to play.

One such visit to her brother-in-law Rueben brought an abrupt end to this 'happy family' pretence. I had been in the 'dog-house' for some weeks because I had contracted mumps and spent Christmas 1949 and the New Year in bed, thus wrecking Olwen's social plans for the holiday. Instead of making the family rounds, she was forced to remain at home, tending to me.

Rueben, who ran a small engineering company, had a son called Cedric, and I had spent the afternoon in his room, playing with his Hornby train set, while the adults were downstairs. When we got back to Chessington around 7.30 pm there was a telephone call from Rueben who told Olwen and my father that he was missing £500, the next week's wages for his staff, which he had left in an envelope on the chest of drawers in his bedroom.

He had quizzed Cedric, who denied all knowledge of the money, so he suggested it must have been me who had taken it. For the rest of the evening I was grilled, threatened with all manner of punishments, then grilled again as to where I had hidden the cash.

Flights of Inspiration

My bedroom was searched twice, as were all my clothes, and anything else that might hold a packet containing £500.

Nothing was found ,because nothing had been taken, and if it had , I certainly wasn't the culprit. Olwen refused to believe my innocence, continually declaring "That's the last straw, he has got to go."

The next morning Rueben rang again to say that the panic was over. He had found the missing money in the safe at his office. He was sorry for any trouble he had caused , but he had forgotten he had put it there.

Neither Olwen ,nor my father, said anything further about the matter. Perhaps they were too embarrassed to apologise to a 12 year old. Instead they got Avril to tell me Rueben's missing money had been found.

Chapter 23
FULL CIRCLE

My 13th birthday came and went without much fuss. My father bought me a new pair of football boots because my old ones were too small. I spent a week softening the hard leather and rigid toecaps by soaking them in hot water, then applying dollops of dubbin.

Otherwise it was the same routine, except that after tea I would spend the evenings in my bedroom, doing homework, then reading books I had borrowed from the school library. When school football finished at the end of the Spring term, I found a new diversion at the weekends. I became a train-spotter.

Together with two or three other boys in the Close I would walk the mile or so to Tolworth station, purchase a one penny platform ticket, then take the electric train to Clapham Junction. This was where the main lines from Victoria and Waterloo converged before fanning out to

Flights of Inspiration

serve South Coast towns like Brighton and Portsmouth, and the West Country.

Steam engines pulled the express trains and we collected their names and numbers in exercise books. The highlights of any day were the arrival of the Golden Arrow at full speed on its way from Victoria to Dover , or the equally fast Brighton Belle with its brown and cream Pullman carriages bearing girls' names.

After a day on the platforms , sustaining ourselves with chocolate from the station vending machines, we would make the return journey to Tolworth, hand in our platform tickets, and walk home comparing the numbers and names we had logged in our books. The railway staff must have known about our dodge to avoid the real fares, but no one ever stopped us. I guess they thought train-spotting kept us from hanging around street corners and getting into mischief.

A few weeks after Easter 1950 my father asked me if I would like to have a holiday. I could go and visit my mother at Leysdown at the Whitsun half term. He had been in touch with her, she had agreed, and would meet me off the train at Sittingbourne. I felt it wasn't so much an inquiry, more of an instruction. I was going whether I wanted to or not.

On the day of my departure he drove me to Charing Cross, bought me a ticket, and put me and my little case on the train to Dover. When I leaned out of the carriage window to say goodbye he told me that I was to ask my mother if I could stay with her permanently. I was not to come back to Chessington.

I looked at the ticket he had given me. It was a single one-way, London to Sittingbourne. He was being serious. Olwen had got her way. I had to go. and now I was going. The worst thing about it was that I had left behind my new football boots.

Mum and Charlie met me at Sittingbourne with hugs and kisses and a warm handshake. They had driven there from Leysdown and we were going to have lunch before making the return journey. First they were going to buy me a present. I was 13 years and two months old, and still in short trousers.

We walked from the train station up to the High Street and I was taken into a menswear shop where I was fitted with a pair of long grey flannels, size 28 waist and 28 inside leg. Suddenly I felt all grown up!

By the time we reached Leysdown memories were flooding back. Mum told me that I now had a sister called Carol who would be four in December, and I would meet Charlie's son John who was just 15, and was also on holiday from school that week.

The biggest surprise was to find Granny Clarke working in the kitchen of the Rose and Crown. She had sold Kandalah in Queens Road, Minster, and moved into a cottage in Leysdown, a short walk from the pub. She cooked meals and kept the house clean, while Mum and Charlie concentrated on the main business.

After a week of being thoroughly spoilt Mum asked me what day I was due to go back. The moment I was dreading had arrived. I started by telling her I didn't know, because I didn't have a railway ticket. Then I blurted out what my father had told me to say.

In three days I was due back at school in Epsom, and there simply wasn't time over the weekend to make the necessary arrangements for a new school and another new home. In fact it was to take a lot longer than anybody thought.

Mum and Charlie had married in August 1947 at Sheppey Register Office, eight months after the birth of Carol. The question of my custody and upbringing to the age of 18 had been a judge's ruling, and neither party could alter the arrangements without applying to the divorce court. Then there was the matter of finding a place at the nearest grammar school, to which I was entitled because of my eleven-plus success. That was something for the Kent Education committee to decide.

Until these issues were resolved I had to return to Chessington and complete the summer term at Epsom. Mum and Charlie took me to Sheerness and bought me a ticket to Tolworth, saying they had spoken to my father and that I was not to worry. They would contact him again when everything was settled.

I will never forget the mixture of surprise and horror on Olwen's face when she answered my knock on the door of Number 12 when I returned to Chessington. What's he doing here "? she screamed at my father, who had emerged from the living room at the sound of her hysterics. Then she slammed the door in my face.

I sat on the doorstep for perhaps half an hour while my father placated her. Eventually I was allowed in and he told me to go up to my bedroom while he sorted things out.

I suppose it was about this time that I lost respect for him. He was a well built man, good-looking and just under six feet. He had come unscathed through six years of war, and I wanted to be proud of him, yet he never seemed capable of facing up to problems, and always took the line of least resistance.

Neither did he take any interest in my progress at school, and never came to watch me play football or cricket, like the other boys' parents. He had started the war as a private in the R.A.S.C. and ended it with the same rank. Yet he was the life and soul of any party, and flirted with all the attractive women.

I saw out the rest of the term without much enthusiasm. Surprisingly the atmosphere at home improved considerably. Olwen became almost pleasant because she knew she was eventually going to get her way, and even Avril began talking to me.

I was out playing with the rest of the boys and girls in the Close when the news that I was waiting for arrived. Everything had been settled, and I would be leaving for Sheppey at the end of the week.

I sorted out the things I wanted to take with me, packing them into my little brown suitcase, alongside my precious football boots. On the last Saturday of July 1950 I happily set out clutching another one-way train ticket. In my pocket was a brand new brown ten-shilling note that my father had given me as a parting gift.

Chapter 24
THAT'S ENTERTAINMENT

I took the train all the way to Sheerness, walked the short distance to the Maidstone and District terminus to catch a bus to Leysdown, and 25 minutes later got off at the stop opposite the Rose and Crown. It was late afternoon, but the village was full of people, of whom a large number were waiting for the pub doors to open at 6.00pm.

On my holiday visit I had not been conscious of just how many changes there had been since I had been taken away by my father at the end of 1945. They soon became obvious. By the time I had met Mum and Charlie, unpacked my case in one of the top floor bedrooms, and ate a late tea prepared by Granny Clarke , the pub was swarming with customers.

In the five years since the end of WW2 Charlie had turned a quiet village inn into a thriving business, and a major centre of attraction for the holiday-makers who were thronging in increasing numbers to Leysdown. They were mostly Londoners, from the East end, as well as South of the river, and being a Londoner himself, Charlie knew exactly what they wanted.

As well as day-trippers and weekenders, whole families would head for Leysdown for a week or fortnight's holiday that was affordable in those austere post-war summers when rationing was still in force. In the years between the two World wars it had been a trickle of bird-watchers and hardy campers who had pitched their tents on the council- run grassland known as Nutts Farm ,with the occasional family hiring a chalet or converted omnibus.

Now it was a flood of pleasure seekers, as those who had survived the horrors of the Blitz, doodle-bugs and V2 rockets, went in search of light relief for the price of a week's wage. They worked hard, and they wanted to enjoy their leisure time. Billy, later Sir Billy, Butlin was one of the first to recognise and meet this demand, and Charlie Arnold was quick to follow suit, albeit on a much smaller scale.

On one side of the Rose and Crown was a one-acre field which he first leased, then purchased. It was roughly 100 yards long and 40 yards wide, and down each side there were ten or 12 chalets and caravans, At the bottom was a large charabanc capable of sleeping eight, and also containing a lounge and small kitchen. It was called

"Hatters Castle" and was owned by actor James Hayter, well known for his portrayal of the Dickens character Mr Pickwick.

Drinking water was available from a standpipe, and there was a small toilet block with washing facilities for the use of the campers. The area down the middle of the field was mown regularly and left free for games. Owners paid an annual rent for their sites.

It was a concept that other local entrepreneurs like Alf Hart, Alf Ives, Ken Butcher, and the Purvis brothers followed, and led directly to the "caravan city" that Leysdown has become today.

In addition Charlie had turned the grounds around the Rose and Crown into a beer garden complete with a 40 x 40 foot wooden stage that served as a dance floor. Around the perimeter were open-fronted "cabins" , the backs and roofs made out of sheets of corrugated iron painted bright blue, complete with wooden benches for seating, and rustic picnic tables.

Lighting was provided by strings of coloured light bulbs attached to the fascias of the cabins, and hung around the dance floor. A dozen or so upturned, empty beer barrels provided additional "parking space" for glasses and empty beer bottles.

Flights of Inspiration

By 7.30 each summer evening it was standing room only, with both the long public bar, and smaller saloon, packed to capacity , and whole families from toddlers in prams to grandparents, occupying the cabins. Children under 18 were not allowed inside the pub, so fathers would buy drinks for the whole family at the bar, then take them on trays to their wives and youngsters sitting outside . In high summer there would be in excess of 1000 holiday-makers either inside or outside the pub.

Music, played through two loudspeakers attached to a shed at the rear of the stage, kept the customers entertained and the children occupied, at least until the adult dancing began around 9.00 pm.

Charlie soon made it clear that I was not to be a spectator of this joyous scene. I was expected to "earn my keep", like everyone else living or working in the house. Because I was too young to be a barman, or even help keep the shelves stocked, I became a disc jockey, sharing the job with Charlie's younger son John.

The discs were nothing like the DVD's or CD's that my grandchildren are so familiar with. They were Bakelite, later vinyl 78's which we played on an ancient record-player wired to the two speakers . Most of them were so well worn and scratched that the needles either skipped a couple of revolutions or jumped sideways, distorting the sound. On top of that the little steel needles wore out quickly and had to be changed regularly.

Nevertheless John and I kept the music going, starting the evening with a mixture of children's tunes and family items like "The Okey-Cokey", then following with Cockney favourites like the Lambeth Walk and Knees Up Mother Brown. In between there were bursts of Vera Lynn wartime classics like Bluebirds over the White Cliffs of Dover.

The hit song of 1950 was My Foolish Heart and that used to get about ten spins a night, until someone came to the shack and said 'please- not that one again'. Frankie Laine was a great favourite and his Mule Train , and Jezebel got many an airing, as did High Noon and I Believe in subsequent summers. However they were almost impossible to dance to, so were interspersed with copious quantities of Victor Sylvester's strict tempo music.

Both John and I found his style boringly repetitive , so everyone now and again we would slip in a jazz recording by Ken Collyer or something from the Glen Miller repertoire. In any case we always ended the evening, when the bars closed at 10.30, with Moonlight Serenade and the Last Waltz.

Afterwards both of us would help collect glasses and empty bottles that had been left in the beer garden, then crawl into bed at 11.00 pm. On Sunday nights, when we finished half an hour earlier ,we would desperately try to stay awake so that we could listen to Jack Jackson's Top 20 record show on Radio Luxembourg.

August raced by, and soon it was time to go back to school. My transfer from Epsom had been confirmed, and I was to join Class 3A at Borden Grammar in Sittingbourne.

Chapter 25
SHOOTING STARS

Although the pioneer fliers and their successors of the RAF had long since departed from Leysdown and Eastchurch, there was still plenty of aerial activity in the skies over Sheppey.

When flying conditions were good, and the sea at low tide, the road from Leysdown to Muswell Manor and the old Shell Beach airfield was closed, red flags were hoisted, and the area became a firing range.

Spitfires and Typhoons from RAF Manston would sweep in at low level unleashing cannon shells and rockets at two large wooden targets anchored offshore . Their marksmanship was recorded and the targets maintained by a small RAF detachment housed in the handful of Nissen huts that remained from the war¬time camp.

It made for noisy and spectacular entertainment for us village boys, who either ran, or cycled, to the barrier across the road to get a closer look. We all wanted to be fighter pilots, even more so when the ageing WW2 planes gave way to the much faster new Meteor jets.

A love of aviation was certainly strong in the Arnold family of which I was now part, if not in name. Charlie's eldest son Dennis had gained his wings at the age of 22, just as hostilities had ended, while his twin sister Eileen had been engaged to a fighter pilot before marrying a Canadian airman.

John was determined that he would join the RAF when he left school, and did so in 1951 when he signed on for 15 years as an apprentice technician. In the meantime I kept my feet on the ground , a necessity considering the journey I had to make to and from school each weekday.

The Kent Education Committee had sent me a rail season ticket which carried me to and from Sittingbourne without charge. The journey involved using the Sheppey Light Railway from Leysdown to Queenborough where I would transfer to the train from Sheerness to Sittingbourne. When I arrived there was a one and a half mile walk from the station via the High Street to Borden School in Remembrance Avenue.

Michael D. Britten

The first train left at 7.30 am after delivering its cargo of milk churns, fresh bread and papers, and consisted of two carriages with hard wooden seats and a guard's van , pulled by a small tank engine. There was only ever a handful of passengers, and as I was the only boy in Leysdown who attended the grammar school, I was sometimes the only person on board, apart from the engine driver and the guard.

This curious ensemble chugged along at a top speed of 40 mph, crossing and re-crossing what is known as the Lower Road, stopping at 'stations' that were little more than a few planks on concrete pillars, plus a shed, and a couple of name signs. The first was Harty Road, which was about four miles from the Ferry Inn at Harty itself, then came Eastchurch and Brambledown Halt, before Minster and East Minster, then Sheerness East. Sometimes people got on and off, and a few workers went all the way to Queenborough, or like me transferred onto the train to Sittingbourne.

This line had been running since 1901, serving the rural community, but not the main bulk of the population who lived in Sheerness and the villages on the northern ridge . One of its idiosyncrasies was that on the homeward trip the driver always waited, especially in bad weather, for the connecting train to arrive at Queenborough in case there were customers for "all stations to Leysdown." Often I was the only passenger.

Much as I appreciated its quaint simplicity, and convenience in delivering me almost to the front door of the Rose and Crown, its days were obviously numbered, and it was no surprise when it closed down at the end of 1950.

Ironically its last train was packed to capacity in both directions as the islanders 'celebrated' its demise with much pomp and ceremony.

Rose and Crown 1934

Leysdown Rd 1934

Santa Maria Pupils 1942 (Author Standing in second row, right)

John Arnold 1951

Bournemouth GS first year 1948

Sgt Pilot Dennis Arnold

To BILL
Dennis Arnold

Newly-weds Dennis and Daphne March 1947

Leysdown FC 1950

Station Road 1950

Chapter 26
MAROONED

Soon afterwards the weather turned bitterly cold, and in early January 1951 heavy snowfalls cut Leysdown off from the rest of the island, as huge drifts obliterated the exposed road to Eastchurch and made the area of Jenkin's Hill impassable. It was more than three weeks before a snow-plough got through, followed by an Army lorry laden with fresh bread and milk for the 300 shivering villagers.

There was no central heating at the Rose and Crown, so it was a very bleak winter as we struggled to keep warm. To augment our dwindling coal supply, John and I were detailed to comb the beach, gathering up driftwood and anything else that would burn. Opposite the pub was The Spinney, which Charlie also owned, and that too was plundered for brushwood, but the elm and oak trees were left standing because of preservation orders. Fortunately we had a good supply of tinned food and soups, but the shelves were almost bare in Leysdown's two provisions shops when the snow-plough arrived.

By the time I had recovered from a subsequent bout of influenza I had missed 41 days of the Spring term at Borden, and more frustratingly Leysdown FC had not played a match in the Sheppey League for more than eight weeks.

I had gained a place in the Borden second XI the previous term, but the school switched to Hockey in the Spring, so I was keen to play football for the village team.

We were a motley bunch. I was nearly 14, but the next youngest was almost twice my age, and our captain, goalkeeper Vic Stutchbury was 50. He always wore a flat cap and handmade sweater, with Leysdown FC embroidered on the front. He was so big he could wrap one of his huge hands around his crossbar without taking either foot off the ground.

I was put on the right wing, well away from the agricultural tackling that was the main feature of inter-village rivalry. Our "home" ground was a stretch of sheep pasture opposite the turning to Warden Bay, about half a mile before the village. There was no pavilion or dressing room, so we either changed into our kit at home, or in a lean-to sheep shelter where the square wooden goalposts were stored.

As in most football of the time goal nets were a luxury, and there were regular disputes over whether the ball had gone between or outside the posts. Sometimes the appointed referee didn't turn up, and in such an emergency one of the few spectators deemed to be impartial, would be prevailed upon to officiate in the interests of keeping the peace. We weren't very good, but we usually managed to win the fiercely fought local 'derbies' against Eastchurch.

With the Light railway closed, new arrangements were made for my daily trek to school. A taxi from Douglas Beard's garage at Eastchurch was sent to collect me at 7.00 am each morning. It deposited me outside the Crooked Billet pub from where I caught the 7.25 am bus to Sheerness, then took the same train that I had previously joined at Queenborough. On the return journey I would take the bus from Sheerness all the way to Leysdown.

Often the taxi would be late, either because of mechanical trouble, or because Mr Beard had overslept. As the bus filled up rapidly with workmen and schoolchildren on its way to Sheerness, he could not risk dropping me ahead of it, so often I was taken all the way in the back of his ancient, but still luxurious Mercedes.

Sometimes I was at Sheerness station so early I had time for coffee and toast in a nearby cafe before the

Michael D. Britten

train for Sittingbourne left at 8.00 am, making up for the breakfast I had not had time to prepare and eat before I left home. Then I caught up with homework I had neglected, by doing it on the train, or cribbing the answers from classmates.

Chapter 27
WITHOUT THE CROWDS

By the end of October each year the last holiday-makers had gone , leaving Leysdown to its own devices. For those villagers who were involved in the leisure business it was time to relax on a holiday of their own, or prepare for the forthcoming season.

The Rose and Crown was the focal point of the village, situated at the junction of the road from Sheerness and Station Road which ran for about 200 yards down towards the seafront. In 1950 these were the only two surfaced roads , the others were unmade.

Hart's general store , containing a small cafe ,was on the pub's left side, and there was a Post Office containing a grocery section, and Payne's newsagents on the left side of Station Road before the railway station At the bottom, next to the seafront were the Sea Horse tea rooms.

Charlie's Spinney occupied the top half of the right side of Station Road, then came a greengrocer's shop which stood alone, and after a large open space there were a couple of gift shops, and right on the seafront an old coastguard station which had been converted into a miniature Butlin's -style camp by an ex-army Major.

There were four or five acres of land behind Alf Hart's shop which contained a large number of converted buses and caravans , while behind the Station were fields of similar size where caravans and Bell tents were pitched

Beyond the village towards the hamlet of Shellness was Nutts Farm, a Council-run facility where pitches could be rented by the day, week, or month. All these camping areas were furnished with rudimentary toilet blocks and spartan wash-houses that dispensed only cold water.

But that didn't deter the thousands of Londoners who flocked to the village where they knew they could enjoy a week's family holiday for less than £20.

A pint of mild ale cost one shilling, bitter and stout a few pennies more. A packet of cigarettes could be bought for one shilling and sixpence, or seven and a half pence in today's money. For ten shillings (50p) a night a man could drown his sorrows or be as happy as a lark.

There were very few excesses. Family discipline was strong ,and drunkenness was regarded with disdain by men and women who knew how to hold their liquor. They ensured the younger element behaved themselves. Few were prepared to cross burly dockers and street market porters.

It was against this happy-go-lucky background that Leysdown expanded year by year. The gaps in Station Road were gradually filled in, first by the establishment of an amusement arcade run by entrepreneur Stan Northover and his wife Eileen, then by more gift shops and cafes.

When the Northovers first arrived with plans for an arcade with slot machines and a bingo stall, many villagers were horrified. Some tried to organise a petition aimed at the removal of such travelling showmen. Their efforts made Stan even more determined to stay. He borrowed money from Charlie to purchase more fruit machines, and found a staunch ally when he repaid the advance in half the time agreed.

Charlie , who was Chairman of the Parish Council, and had a say in much of the new development, was also expanding his sphere of activity. The bus company had acquired a piece of land to the east of the village, wherein their vehicles could park while their crews took rest breaks before commencing the return journey to Sheerness,

Opposite this makeshift bus terminus were a pair of cottages next to the Village Hall, and a wedge of land, behind which lay Wing Road. Charlie purchased this plot and had a building constructed and fitted out as Wing Cafe., which Dennis and Daphne began to operate, while living in one of the adjacent cottages.

At the same time Charlie purchased a vacant building plot on the other side of Wing Road, where he later had Wing House constructed, and also a two acre meadow beyond the Village Hall, which was subsequently transformed into Wing Holiday Camp.

Now bus crews could have breakfast, lunch, and tea, or a snack and hot drink during their turn-around, and more importantly, so could departing holiday-makers. This area became progressively more important, and profitable ,as the village spread outwards to accommodate new caravan and camping areas.

Chapter 28
ARTISTIC LICENCE

The coming of winter was the signal for Charlie and Bebe, as Mum had now become universally known because of her former initials, to resume their weekly Tuesday visits to Maidstone Market. He simply could not resist a bargain and the pub's garage was crammed so full of them he could barely put his car away.

Two of his oddest purchases were six twenty-gallon drums of yellow paint and 100 cases of un-labelled baked beans that were sold as Army-surplus.

Every night when I came home from school I knew what tea would consist of. Granny Clarke did her best to disguise the menu by sometimes cooking a poached egg to go on top , or adding scrambled eggs on toast, but there is a limit to the variations on a can of beans. It got to the stage where I would spend some of my hard-earned ten shillings a week pocket money on a snack in a cafe in Sheerness , then tell Gran I was not hungry when I got home. Anything to avoid baked beans!

The paint was used to change the colour of the cabins in the beer garden. It took three of us, John, myself and the potman Sonny Boy Wade, the best part of a month to obliterate the original sky blue, and we had not even started on the second drum. The result was horrendous. It was such an assault on the optic nerves that you needed sun-glasses to prevent a blinding headache. Even Charlie was forced to admit he might have made an error of judgment.

As he had paid only £10 for the six drums and a further £5 delivery charge it was no big deal. But we had to spend another month re-painting the woodwork blue, leaving only the backs and roofs coloured yellow. It was still garish, but much easier on the eye, especially after dark.

At half term, and in the school holidays, John and I would sometimes accompany Charlie and Bebe to Maidstone. After the ritual tour of the market and the obligatory purchases ,we would take a picnic lunch on the River Medway if the weather was good, hiring a rowing boat which John and I would crew.

The winter months were a total contrast to the hectic summer. The opening hours were the same, but during the week only one half of the public bar was in use. A roaring fire kept it cosy and warm on the coldest nights, although often only six or seven locals would call in for a drink, and if the weather was really bad, none at all.

My sister Carol was too young to stay up late, but after John went off to join the RAF I would join Charlie and Bebe in the bar, and play darts or cribbage, or just chat with the regulars until going to bed around 10 pm. We would toast currant tea-cakes on the fire and sometimes there would be a loaf, a bread knife, and a bowl of dripping, together with a jar of pickled onions, on the counter for the benefit of hungry customers.

We were all reasonably proficient at darts which was played on a Kentish board. It did not have trebles, so no one ever heard the cry of "One hundred and eighty" because it could not be achieved. We played legs of 301 instead of 501, and bull's eye (50) or 'double top' (double 20) were the highest scores possible. In addition to hand-eye co-ordination, the secret of good play was speed in mental arithmetic which allowed a player to calculate what double was required to win a game, without breaking throwing rhythm.

Occasional darts matches against pubs from Eastchurch and Minster helped to while away the long evenings, and there was a fortnightly whist drive in the Village Hall. Charlie had converted a small tea-room on the right hand side of the pub into a games room which contained another of his Maidstone

Market purchases, a medium sized snooker table. Many an evening was spent in there with boys from the village. By the age of 16, I had a good grounding in at least two of the major vices!

Weekends were slightly busier as a few caravan and chalet owners arrived to do maintenance work on their holiday homes, then came Christmas and New Year when up would go the decorations and the season of goodwill brought most of the villagers in for a celebratory drink at one time or another.

Then the yearly cycle would begin all over again, with everybody eagerly awaiting Easter and the advance guard of chalet and caravan owners, that signalled another hectic summer was approaching.

Chapter 29
COCKLES AND MUSSELS

By the mid-1920's Eustace and Oswald Short were in charge of a thriving company, that had become an integral part of British aviation. They were building reliable, sturdy aircraft that were in great demand, and when they brought out the tiny Cockle single-seat flying boat in 1924 it heralded a revolutionary method of construction.

This was the first aircraft built entirely of metal with a stressed-skin fuselage of aluminium. It had two major advantages over the previous wood and fabric design. Firstly its component parts could be stamped out of sheet metal, thus speeding up the production process, and secondly it overcame the problem of wooden hulls becoming waterlogged.

The Cockle had a wing span of only 34 feet, and was powered by two 16 horse power motor cycle engines, giving it a top speed of only 65 mph, but it was to lead Shorts to much greater things.

Although their custom-built seaplane works at Rochester was the centre of this activity, Eustace and Oswald never forgot their humble beginnings at Muswell Manor. When in 1926 there became a need for a small plane in which they could test their theories, they built two which they named Mussel 1 and Mussel 2, after the Manor on the marshes near Leysdown.

The Mussels were basically more powerful versions of the Cockle, and were two-seaters. They became popular as a light touring seaplane largely because of Eustace's belated interest in flying. He had turned 50 when John Lankester Parker, his chief test pilot, took him up for his first flight.

By October 1927 he had gone solo, and thereafter spent as much time as he could in the air, particularly relishing the experience of flying in rough weather.

However in August the following year he was coming into land on the Medway after a solo flight, when a wing tip struck the mast of a barge and Mussel 1 cart-wheeled into the river.

Eustace was rescued unhurt, but both wings had been torn off the plane, and its chassis and tail had been

Flights of Inspiration

buckled. When it was taken back to the workshops for examination it was deemed beyond repair .

Orders were given for the production of Mussel 2 which was an improved version of the original, with a more powerful engine, and the addition of water rudders to make taxiing easier. John Parker tested it in May 1929 and Eustace, his nerve still intact, resumed flying with such enthusiasm that by February 1931 he had completed more than 200 hours solo, and passed his "A" licence.

Subsequently he flew almost daily until April 8th, 1932 when he suffered a fatal heart attack just after he made a perfect touch down close to the Rochester works. Onlookers realised something was wrong when the seaplane continued taxiing, and grounded in the mud on the London side of the river, because Eustace had not been able to switch off the ignition.

He was buried in Hampstead Cemetery in north London, alongside elder brother Horace, leaving Oswald as the new head of Shorts. He was to lead them to even greater achievements, most notably with the Short Kent, then the S23 "C" , better known as the Empire flying boat, operated by Imperial Airways.

More than any other plane it brought romance into air travel. It could accommodate 17 passengers in comfort and safety, as well as luggage and mail, and became the mainstay of Imperial's services, after they had given Shorts an order worth £1.75 million to build 28 of them for use on their Empire routes.

Two later versions of this aircraft operated the first scheduled airline flights across the Atlantic from Ireland to Newfoundland in 1937. These flying boats gave Britain a domination of civil air routes that might have been unchallenged but for the outbreak of WW2 . As it transpired, the Empire design was turned to military advantage, it being fundamentally that which Shorts employed in the production of the legendary U-boat hunter , the Sunderland flying boat.

Chapter 30
GOING UNDERGROUND

When Charlie Arnold first took over the Rose and Crown it was owned by George Beer and Rigden, a small family brewery based in Faversham.

Although their headquarters was probably no more than five miles away as the crow flies, it took the best part of a day for one of their wheezy steam lorries to make the return journey by road via Sittingbourne, and the ancient bridge on to the Isle of Sheppey.

That did not matter so much in the pre-war years, when one or two deliveries each week would suffice. But once the holiday trade began to mushroom in the post-war years, Rigdens found great difficulty in keeping up with the volume of trade Charlie had achieved at the Rose and Crown.

It came as no great surprise when in 1948 they were taken over by the much larger Fremlin's Company, whose brewery in Earl Street, Maidstone was close to the market. Their delivery vehicles were modern articulated lorries which could each carry a ten-ton load. During the busiest weeks in summer , one or sometimes two, would arrive early every morning.

Unloading the 36 gallon barrels of mild or bitter beer and dozens of crates of light and brown ale, and stout, was a major operation which needed to be completed before the pub doors were open for business. While the draymen did the heavy work, transferring the full barrels down the ramp into the cellar under the public bar, the potman Sonny Boy and us lads, piled crates of beer on to trolleys, and wheeled them to the beer store at the rear of the pub. On the return trip we brought back crates of empties to load on to the lorry.

It was hard physical labour, but many hands made light work, and in little more than an hour a lorry was emptied and re-loaded before everyone took a well-earned break. When the empties had been tallied, and the draymen had departed, the second stage of the operation began.

As the barmaids began arriving for their 10.30 am start, Sonny Boy and his team of helpers would start transferring full crates from the store and begin the task of emptying them on to the bar shelves. At the same time Charlie would be down in the cellar ensuring there

Flights of Inspiration

would be no shortage of top quality draught beer at the bar pumps.

Shortly after my 15th birthday during the Easter holiday, he plucked me from the trolley-pulling gang for my first lesson in cellar-work. The door was sited in the hallway, which also contained the coin-box public telephone behind the entrance to the saloon bar, and a steep flight of steps led down to where the barrels were stored.

There was a single bare bulb dangling from the ceiling, but most of the light came from the trapdoors which opened on to the forecourt. Steps led up to ground level and a wooden ramp enabled barrels to be lowered by rope and tackle ,or pushed up when empty.

The barrels were mounted horizontally, side by side on wooden cradles called stalters which were curved at each end to match their circular shape. From a tap at the front transparent plastic tubes led through a hole in the ceiling to the bar pump. In the early days these tubes had been made entirely of lead !

Each barrel theoretically contained 288 pints. In practice a good publican would expect to lose only two or three per cent, and that would be the sediment at the bottom of the barrel which was known as ullage. As a barrel emptied, the next one would be connected, and the empty rolled up the cellar ramp to do duty as a table top on the forecourt, or in the beer gardens.

Charlie showed me the technique of tapping and spiling a barrel to prepare it for use, and how to disconnect the plastic tubes and wash them through with warm soapy water. Tapping involved driving a metal tap into the large bung on the front of the barrel by means of a wooden or rubber mallet. Spiling was a similar operation, using a small tapered wooden peg which was tapped into a vent on the roof of the barrel and then left loose to allow gas to escape.

It would take two, sometimes three days, before the beer that had been shaken around in the delivery process, would settle, and be ready to be drawn at the pump. Each morning the floor would be hosed down so that the cellar remained scrupulously clean.

The art of the good cellar man was to ensure that the supply to the pumps remained uninterrupted and of the best quality, by judging when to manoeuvre the full barrels on to the stalters, and when to tap and spile the ones already there.

Devotees of real ale will be aware of this procedure, but most of today's modern bars have long dispensed with the old ways. Steel canisters of bland, carbonated lager are now the norm.

Charlie and Sonny Boy also showed me how to manoeuvre a full barrel into position by finding its centre of balance and rolling it on its rim. I also learnt the knack of stacking crates up to eight or ten high, well above my head. Physical work yes, but more interesting than putting on the same records night after night.

Chapter 31
THE SHIRT

It did not take me long to realise why I had been introduced to the arcane arts of the potman. Only occasionally did Sonny Boy work in the evenings, his usual hours were from 8-6, not including Sundays. So it was prudent of Charlie to have a replacement available should he not want to leave the bars and tend to the cellar.

My presence as an auxiliary potman also gave him the opportunity to indulge his penchant for showmanship, when he had a mind to entertain the customers.

Our nearest neighbours were Alf and Sue Ives, who had a large house behind the Rose and Crown with a small caravan park attached. In their field they kept a white horse which had been bought as a pony for their daughters Fay and Rene. The novelty had worn off and

Flights of Inspiration

it was ridden only rarely. The animal spent most of its time munching hay, and providing manure for Sue's rose garden.

Alf was only too happy to oblige when Charlie inquired whether it needed exercise, and if so, could he borrow it occasionally during the evenings. It made its debut as one of the Rose and Crown's attractions early in June 1952, and was greeted with such enthusiasm that it became an integral part of the evening entertainment.

Around 9.30 pm three or four times a week, Alf would saddle the horse and lead it through a gap in the hedge between the two properties and into our backyard where Charlie would be waiting in his ringmaster's outfit.

This consisted of a pair of boots and corduroy trousers into which was tucked a brightly coloured shirt. Around his waist was a belt with two toy pistols in their holsters, and on his head was a white ten gallon Stetson. He looked like a cross between Hopalong Cassidy and Tom Mix, two Western stars of the Saturday morning pictures which children used to frequent in those days.

Charlie would hoist two empty crates, connected by a short rope, over the pommel of the saddle so that they rested on each side of the horse. He then mounted the animal and rode it around the beer garden, inviting dozens of excited children to collect the empty beer bottles and deposit them in the crates.

The kids loved it of course, scurrying around picking up the 'empties' , and urging their parents to 'drink up' so that they could put more bottles into the crates. This would last for half an hour or so, before the horse was returned to its field to eat more grass.

Along with most of the "workers" I used to regard it as just a bit of harmless self indulgence from someone who would have made an excellent showman. Then I realised there was method in Charlie's cowboy antics.

For years the Rose and Crown had been the focal point of the village, and the sole attraction for those who liked a drink and a bit of fun. But that was beginning to change with the growth of holiday camps whose proprietors realised that they too could tap into this lucrative market, by offering similar facilities. They began erecting clubhouses containing seating and dancing areas, and obtaining licenses to serve alcoholic drinks.

Charlie's "Wild West Show" was his way of keeping his clientele. It would be a hard-hearted father who could resist his child's pleas to see the 'man on the horse' collecting beer bottles. Thus the crowds kept on coming.

Later on Charlie took to riding around the village on summer afternoons when the pub was closed, steering a cart drawn by a donkey, with Bebe sitting alongside him.

Flights of Inspiration

In return for the use of his horse, Charlie allowed Alf and Sue to park their seafood stall on the pub forecourt free of charge. It remained there for many years, selling cockles and whelks, and Alf's speciality, bowls of jellied eels, which were a big favourite of the East Enders.

It was from the latter that Charlie got most of the material for his gaudy shirts.

Occasionally a pearly King and Queen in full Cockney regalia, would be among the holiday-makers and he would ask them to keep an eye out for unusual cloth, which he would have made up by a seamstress in the village, when they brought it down on their next trip. Sometimes people who had been abroad would bring a length of brilliantly coloured material, which he would add to his wardrobe.

Occasionally he would receive a postcard or letter addressed simply "The Shirt", Leysdown, England, which he would display on the mirror-backed shelves in the saloon bar.

Chapter 32
GROUND TO AIR MISSILES

The exercise involved in stacking crates and shifting barrels had given me greater upper body strength than was usual for boys of my age. Although I wasn't tall, I was stocky and fit, and could hold my own in senior football, which I had been playing with the village team in the Sheppey League.

Cricket was my second love, and Athletics a distant third. Football had taught me to be very quick over the first 20 or 30 yards, but other boys were faster over longer distances, so I gave up sprinting and switched to the long jump where I was close to breaking the 20 foot barrier. It was while I was practising my run-up during a morning athletics session that the School Sports Master asked me if I had ever thrown the javelin.

Flights of Inspiration

When I replied in the negative he handed me a ladies model and invited me to throw it. I had no idea of the technique required, so just gripped the handle on the shaft, took a couple of steps and hurled it as far as I could.

He offered to teach me the necessary run up and proper release, and said he would enter me for the forthcoming Swale Athletic Championships. By the time they arrived I could throw the aluminium spear around 150 feet without straining my back, and to my great surprise that was good enough to win the competition. The next week I went to the Kent Schools Championships at Gillingham, and won that as well, with a lesser throw.

Two or three other boys from Borden had also won County titles, and we were sent off to represent Kent in the 1952 English Schools National Championships at Southampton. I was hopelessly out of my depth in both my specialist events, and although I made the top ten, I came home feeling I had let the School down.

It was all the more frustrating a week later, when during an athletics match against Kent College, Canterbury I added a further 20 feet to my previous javelin best, having dashed to the line after completing my three attempts in the long jump competition. Too late had I realised the value of being properly warmed up.

I did better the following year, retaining my county javelin title and going to the National Schools finals at Bradford. But I was nowhere near good enough to win, and I knew I would never be an Olympic athlete!

Cricket was much more rewarding. I opened the batting for the School second XI and gained a place in the First XI for the last two matches of the season where I batted at number nine, and fielded at cover point. I also got the odd chance to play in club cricket for the well known Gore Court club in Sittingbourne, who often called on boys from local schools to make up the numbers in mid-week matches.

One of them I remember particularly well was Brian Luckhurst who was a pupil at Sittingbourne West, and was originally a leg-break bowler who could bat a bit. He went on to became an outstanding opening batsman for Kent and England.

Curiously cricket was not a game that had much of a following on Sheppey, whereas almost every village in the Sittingbourne area had its own side, and there was a strong interest in the fortunes of the Kent county team. It all added to the feeling that although the island had a charm of its own, it was missing out on a lot of the good things in life.

I would not have had much time for weekend cricket anyway, because as soon as the term finished at the end of July it was back to work as junior potman and bar shelves stacker at the Rose and Crown. Pay ten shillings pocket money for a seven day week, and my keep, as Charlie put it.

When I discovered that other boys from the village, and casual hands, were paid two shillings an hour, and got at least one night off per week I began to think it wasn't such a good deal, especially as most of my meals consisted of Army-surplus baked beans. It was time to become a rebellious teenager !

Chapter 33
TIME BOMB

I decided the best way to improve my 'working conditions' was to talk to my mother first. I said I wasn't really interested in the money, but I felt it was unfair that I had to work every day with no time to myself. Privately, I resolved that if Charlie didn't agree to treat me like the rest of the boys, I would go and work for somebody else who would pay me, until it was time to go back to school.

She listened and said she would talk to Charlie. Nothing was said for a week or so then she told me I could have Thursday nights off, and my pocket money would go up to £1 per week. I agreed, but said I didn't want to see any more baked beans.

During the summer weeks there were regular boat trips from Sheerness to Southend to visit the Kursaal amusement park, so on the following Thursday I joined two of the village boys who had already bought tickets. While we were crossing the Thames Estuary I asked one of the crew whether the wreck we had just passed had been sunk by the Germans during the war.

He laughed and said " No way. That was one we sank ourselves, and now we've got to live with it." He did not elaborate and I thought no more of it, until the next morning when I asked Charlie about it. All he knew was that it was an American boat full of high explosives, and it was still dangerous.

Even now more than 60 years since it went down a mile off Sheerness in August 1944, the people of Sheppey are reluctant to discuss the sinking of the USS Richard Montgomery, and the threat she still poses to the island.

This American Liberty ship went aground on a sandbar close to where she had been "parked" while waiting to join a convoy heading for Cherbourg. She was laden with munitions destined for the American forces, who following the D-Day landings, were breaking out of the Cotentin peninsular and driving towards Paris.

There are still over 3000 tonnes of bombs contained in separate sections of the stricken vessel, and no one can be certain that they will not explode with devastating consequences for Sheppey, and other towns on both sides of the Thames Estuary.

The USS Richard Montgomery had arrived in the Thames off Southend on August 19th and came under the control of the Naval establishment operating from Southend Pier. The Harbour Master controlled all shipping in the Estuary, and ordered the boat to anchor off the north end of Sheerness Middle Sand, where there would be between five and six fathoms of water at low tide.

What he did not know was that the Richard Montgomery was not a standard Liberty Ship which had a draught of around 28 feet. Her stern was trimmed to a depth of almost 33 feet, and when on the next day the wind freshened and swung round to the north, she was pushed backwards on to the sandbar where she grounded at high tide.

When the tide ebbed she stuck fast, and very soon her welded plates began to buckle and crack. Local fishermen saw the crew hastily abandoning ship, and the alarm was raised.

Three days later salvage work commenced, with a firm of stevedores from Rochester engaged to carry out the perilous task. The next day there was a transverse crack at the front of the Number Three hold , which led to No 1 and No 2 holds being flooded. The vessel broke her back on September 8th and became permanently stranded.

The stevedores switched their efforts to clearing the rear No 4 and No 5 holds, but the more explosives they removed the more the stern rose, and it eventually broke away from the rest of the vessel. The salvage work continued until September 25th, when the rear holds were emptied and the wreck was abandoned.

Today there are two submerged sections buried in silt and sand. The experts agree that they constitute an explosive hazard but are divided on the danger they constitute to life and property. Some feel the bombs have become safer because of the length of time they have been submerged. Others feel it is a disaster waiting to happen.

They fear that as the bombs have unprotected fuses, they could become highly unstable, if exposed to water vapour. There could be a spontaneous explosion if water penetrates the bombs. At high tide it would create a tidal wave that would swamp Sheppey and other low lying areas in the Estuary, while the blast would cause the level of damage anticipated from a small atom bomb.

The optimists say that nothing has happened for over 60 years and that is support for their theory that the cargo has already deteriorated to safety level, or will continue to do so. They also seek to reassure Sheppey residents by saying that if an explosion occurs, they hope it will be at low tide, which would significantly diminish any tidal wave.

In 1999 a risk assessment was commissioned by the Government, but it has not been published. According to the New Scientist magazine it outlined options for dealing with the problem, one of which involved the burying of the ship in concrete. Another involved removing the cargo, although to do so would involve the evacuation of the 12,000 inhabitants of Sheerness.

Recent operations around the wreck seemed to have been designed to reassure concerned citizens. The masts which had been protruding from the water and rusting away for more than 60 years, have been removed, along with the attached signs warning of danger from unexploded munitions. Presumably on the basis of what the eye doesn't see, the heart doesn't grieve.

But there is no doubt that the authorities remain concerned, for every two years a team of Royal Navy divers goes down to inspect the wreck. In the meantime no one talks, and the people of Sheppey go about their business , as though the time bomb does not exist.

Chapter 34
CAREER OPTIONS

At the end of my first year at Borden I had been asked what I intended to do when I left school. At 14 I had no idea and told my form-master so. One year later I gave the same answer to the same question, but that only led to official concern that I did not seem to have much ambition.

I was called to headmaster George Hardy's study when I returned to school for the start of the fifth year for a serious career talk. I was told to apply my mind to my future, so I responded by telling him that I wanted to be a footballer, and if that didn't turn out , then I aimed to be a fighter pilot.

That seemed to satisfy his need to put me into some sort of pigeon-hole and I thought no more about it until a few weeks later, when he emerged from his house in the corner of the school playing field one Saturday morning, to watch the first XI's football match against Faversham Grammar. After the game he made a point of telling me that football would be a poor choice for a career, because there was no money in a game that was only a working man's recreation.

The following Monday morning I was back in his study to hear him announce " I see you as a naval Lieutenant Commander, and I have entered you for the Dartmouth College Entrance Examination. You will take it in the school library next week under my personal supervision."

I was stunned, and stood there with my mouth open in disbelief. I lived by the sea and liked swimming in it, when it was warm, but I had been very queasy on my boat trip across the Thames Estuary, and mildly seasick on a day trip from Dover to Calais. A life on the ocean wave was definitely not on my agenda.

I knew there was no point in arguing, so I resigned myself to the ordeal. Evidently there weren't any other budding Lieutenant Commanders in the fifth form, so I spent four days alone, apart from the lunch break, sitting in a library I was forbidden to consult, watched over by the Headmaster or his deputy Mr Ashby, as I struggled with a variety of exam papers.

Flights of Inspiration

Each was of three hours duration, and I was told that I had to achieve better than 50 per cent in all of them to qualify for the personal interview stage. I managed my favourite subjects , History, English, Geography, and Languages well enough, and just about coped with Mathematics.

But I was all at sea with the Physics and Science papers, subjects in which I had such little interest that I had exercised my option to drop both at the end of the fourth year. I knew I would definitely be keeping my feet on dry land.

In the meantime John had already decided on his career. He had left school in the summer and signed on for 15 years as an apprentice technician in the Royal Air Force. By the time I had returned to school he had already said his farewells, and started his training at RAF Halton, near Aylesbury.

When the Headmaster expressed his optimism about my Dartmouth College chances in my end of term School Report it triggered further discussion on my future, this time with Mum and Charlie.

He felt strongly that even if I failed the Navy exam, I should consider the Army or RAF. If not I should leave school anyway as soon as I was 16, and get a job. Mum had no particular view, but I did not fancy life in any of the Services, and I suspected that "getting a job" meant, in the short term at least, working full time at the Rose and Crown. Experience had already taught me that Charlie was unlikely to be a generous employer., especially to a member of his family.

Sheppey was something of a depressed area at the time, and almost all my school friends were talking of leaving the island and going to London or elsewhere. I told Mum and Charlie that I wanted to work with my head, not my hands.

A compromise was reached. If I gained five "O" levels in the GCE exams in June 1953, I could stay at school for two further years in the sixth form. If I didn't, I would leave and find a job, either on the island or further a-field.

Chapter 37
THE GREAT FLOOD

On the night of Saturday January 31st 1953 a great storm surge swept down the North Sea and devastated the East coast of England. Caused by a freak combination of hurricane-force winds, a deep depression, and unusually high Spring tides, it resulted in hundreds of deaths , the destruction of 24,000 homes, and the flooding of 200,000 acres, in which thousands of animals were drowned. In Holland there was an even greater catastrophe as over 1800 people were drowned when the raging sea overwhelmed the dykes.

There was no flood warning system in operation at that time, and the citizens in the coastal areas of Lincolnshire were taken unawares when the onrushing sea water swept ashore around 5.00 pm, crushing seaside houses and caravans, and drowning 41 people. The destructive wind had blown down so many telephone lines, that warnings could not be given to counties further south before it was too late.

The tidal wave swept on southwards across the Wash, striking King's Lynn and the coastal towns and villages along the north Norfolk coast. A total of 100 people were drowned in this region as their houses were hit by a six feet wall of water, and most of the county became a vast inland lake. Next the North Sea coasts of Norfolk and Suffolk bore the brunt around midnight, when Felixstowe and Harwich were flooded. Then 35 were drowned at Jaywick Sands near Clacton, before in the early hours of Sunday morning the surge hit the Thames Estuary.

By then the authorities were aware that they had a major natural disaster on their hands, but were powerless to prevent it, and things got worse. As the depression, which had begun forming over the Shetland Islands, moved southwards down the North Sea, the wind reached well over 100 mph, and the height of the surge increased. By the time it arrived in the shallower waters off Essex and Kent it was in the region of ten feet.

The sudden arrival of such a large amount of water in the relatively narrow Thames and Medway estuaries was too much for both the sea walls, and the flimsier sand and shingle defences. Canvey Island on the Essex side was struck in the middle of the night and its sea walls collapsed. Those who survived the initial flood spent hours clinging to roof tops in the bitter cold before they could be rescued by boat. A total of 58 were drowned, along with almost all the livestock. The devastation was so complete that all 13,000 inhabitants were made homeless, and the island had to be evacuated.

The water swept up the Thames and by first light was lapping a few inches below the walls along the Embankment. There was severe flooding from Tilbury all the way to the Pool of London. Factories, and gas and electricity stations serving the capital were put out of action, and the areas around West Ham were inundated when a stretch of the river banking collapsed.

On the south side of the Estuary the oil refinery on the Isle of Grain was flooded, and Sheppey was just as badly hit, although there was no loss of life. The water swept over the sea walls at Sheerness , flooding the Naval Dockyard and the town, and the rest of the low-lying island.. The railway link to the mainland was put out of action when the overflowing Medway combined with the tidal surge to wash away its embankments. Only villages such as Minster, Eastchurch and Warden on higher ground, escaped unscathed. Leysdown was marooned in a lake which stretched as far as the eye could see,

North Kent coastal towns such as Whitstable were flooded, and many rivers broke their banks, but amazingly there was only one fatality in the county.

Across the Channel it was a very different story as the unrelenting North Sea battered the coasts of Belgium and the Netherlands. Over 2000 people were drowned, the majority in Holland, where the sea flooded more than 50 polders. Many more would have lost their lives but for American helicopters, based in Germany, plucking hundreds from their rooftops.

There were also many deaths at sea. The ferry Princess Victoria had left Stranraer early on Saturday morning bound for Larne in Northern Ireland. The ancient car transporter was unfit to cope with the storm that also raced down the Irish Sea, and only 44 of the 172 passengers and crew were saved when she went down. Several smaller boats, including the Lowestoft trawler the Guava ,with eleven men on board, disappeared without trace.

All down the coast from Mablethorpe to Margate there were tales of destruction and despair, as details of the worst disaster of the Century became known. There had been more than 1200 breaches of the sea defences, and the final death toll was 307.

The Rose and Crown was approximately 50 feet above sea level, but water was lapping at the front door, when we went downstairs at first light. Every building in Station Road was flooded , some up to window level, and so were all the bungalows and houses in the unmade roads between the pub and the sea wall. Great chunks of reinforced concrete had been ripped out of the sea wall, and tossed aside like pieces of plywood

Gradually people emerged from their homes, and waded through the flood to congregate at the pub, where Granny Clarke kept the teapot hot and full as we listened to the story of that night of horror unfolding on the radio. A few of the village lads made a tour of the bungalows to check on the elderly. Everyone was accounted for, although they were to spend weeks drying out their homes and possessions because of the flood damage.

Charlie and I spent some time trying to pump two to three feet of water out of the cellar, once we had secured the floating beer barrels, and made sure those in use had not been contaminated. It was a hopeless task. There was a drain in the centre of the cellar floor, but underneath there was an old well. The water-table was so high that as fast as we pumped water out it bubbled up again. We decided to let nature take its course. It took nearly three weeks before the last of the water drained away.

We had got away lightly, but once again Leysdown was cut off from the rest of the island. It was more than a week before a fire engine negotiated the flooded roads to bring fresh milk and food, and much longer before the bus service to and from Sheerness resumed, and the railway line to Sittingbourne reopened.

Chapter 36
CASH AND CARRY

Prime Minister Winston Churchill declared East Anglia a disaster area, and very soon an inquest began into why there had been no warning of the catastrophe, and what could be done to prevent a further disaster of such magnitude.

Decisions were taken to reinforce the sea defences along the whole of the East coast, and build a Thames Barrier to protect London from future flooding. In addition the groundwork was laid for the formation of today's computerised meteorological early warning system. It took another 30 years before the Thames Barrier was constructed at Woolwich and opened in 1984, but work on new sea walls began almost immediately.

The existing sea defences at Leysdown had been badly damaged, and also needed extending. The contract was awarded to the John Mowlem construction group, and just before Easter a work force of nearly 300 mainly Irish labourers descended on the village, where they were billeted in the former RAF camp on the road to Muswell Manor.

Initially they were barely noticeable, but it wasn't long before a few of them began visiting the Rose and Crown at weekends, and causing Charlie and the rest of his staff a major headache. After a week of hard labour from dawn to dusk they were ready to unwind, and eager to spend some of their wages, which were considerable by local standards.

In the early part of the evening they mingled happily enough with the Londoners, but by 10.00 pm many of them were the worse for wear, and ready for a fight, more often than not amongst themselves.

Charlie diffused many a threatening situation by piling the most inebriated into the back of his Lea-Francis shooting brake, and driving them back to the RAF camp, which they would never have reached under their own steam.

After a while they began to regard Charlie's "taxi service" as a perk to which they were entitled. Word spread that a man could go to the pub on a Saturday night, get as drunk as a skunk, and the 'guvnor' would drive him home to sleep it off. Instead of a night in the cells, and a date with the magistrate, he got a free trip back to bed.

Consequently numbers increased at weekends, and inevitably they became involved in arguments with the holiday makers, as well as each other. Many were the potentially explosive situations, and there was rarely any sign of the Constabulary.

The village policeman was Constable "Jock" Cameron, who lived in Eastchurch, and cycled to Leysdown two of three times a week to check all was well on his rural beat. In the winter he would call at the side door of the Rose and Crown on a cold evening, and Charlie would dispense a hot toddy of Scotch and ginger for "medicinal purposes". In the summer when there were drunken Mowlem's men spoiling for a scrap, he was rarely to be seen.

He could hardly be blamed for his caution, because his back-up were his superiors in Sheerness, and they were not exactly eager to get involved in any problems in Leysdown. So Charlie was left on his own to deal with matters as best he could.

He was helped in keeping an uneasy peace by the "gangers" who were foremen in charge of a squad of labourers. One of them, known as "Highland Jock", had a particular reason to ensure his men kept the peace, for the Rose and Crown was also his bank.

Flights of Inspiration

This situation came about when early one Sunday evening he came into the public bar, and asked to have a quiet word with the "Missus". Mum talked to him in a corner of the bar where he handed over an envelope containing £1,000 in cash, which she agreed to look after for him. There was no bank in Leysdown, only a post office, and he needed a safe haven for his money, which he feared was in danger of being stolen from his quarters at the RAF camp.

Others soon followed suit, and Bebe kept a cash book in which she entered the amount deposited by each "investor", none of whom used their real names.

Down the left hand side of the page were a list of aliases like Corky, Whiskey Mac, Dublin Seamus, Limerick Liam, and Little Jimmy, and of course Highland Jock. Alongside was the date and amount of the sums they had paid in, and in the right hand column was the total each was in credit.

The money was kept alongside the pub takings in a safe under the floor boards of the upstairs sitting room. At any one time there was more than £30,000 of the workers' money being held in the "pub-bank". Every now and again one of her customers would come in to say he was "going home for a holiday" and withdraw £500, or sometimes as much as £1,000.

Apart from one pane of glass in the main door to the public bar, the pub remained undamaged throughout the time the Mowlem men were in Leysdown. Occasionally Charlie would remind them that if he had to close it for repairs, the nearest hostelry was four miles away, so "what sort of man would be responsible for depriving his mates of somewhere to drink at the weekend"?

Bebe ran her "bank book" for 18 months until one day a ganger came in to tell her the work on the sea walls was nearly finished and they would all be leaving at the end of the month. Everyone got back what they had put "on deposit", to the exact pound. Her reward was a handsome tip from each customer, much as though they were rewarding a bookmaker who had paid out promptly on an Irish outsider at the Cheltenham National Hunt Festival.

She was glad to be rid of the responsibility, because the strain on her and Charlie had begun to take its toll.

Chapter 37
MOVING ON

The burden of keeping the peace in what became the Coronation year of Queen Elizabeth II, and the advent of his 60th birthday in April, persuaded Charlie that it was nearly time to move on.

The summer of 1953 was as hectic as ever at the Rose and Crown, but slowly and almost imperceptibly Leysdown was changing. More holiday camps had opened for business, and more of them contained clubs where music and other entertainment, as well as alcoholic drinks, were offered to holiday-makers.

Instead of just the pub there were half a dozen "mini pubs" operating during the high summer period, and although the latter had rules which restricted their use to club members, they were largely ignored, and rarely enforced. It became possible to make a "club tour" which appealed to the younger element, and gradually groups of them began to flock to the village.

They came not only from London, but also other parts of the island, and mainland Kent, most often at weekends, but also on day trips. The families kept on coming, and so did Mowlem's men, ready for some hard drinking at the end of a hard working week on the sea walls.

At first it was a harmonious scene, principally because of the lay out of the village. The first clubs were some distance apart, so movement from one to the other sometimes involved a trek of perhaps half a mile or more. Most families tended to stay where they began the evening, then dispersed happily to their caravans and chalets.

The danger period was around 11.00 pm on a Saturday evening after the clubs had closed, when youths congregated at the village centre, and mingled with the Mowlem's men turning out of the Rose and Crown.

A fish and chip shop had replaced the old Tomlin's store demolished by a war-time bomb, and it did a roaring trade in the hour before midnight.

As most of its clientele were well lubricated when they arrived for their "supper", it soon became a potential flashpoint, especially as our village policeman was, as usual, somewhere else. The first serious trouble erupted on a Saturday night in August, when one of the Mowlem's men picked up one of the young revellers, and bodily threw him through the plate glass window of Greeno's fish and chip emporium.

A free-for-all ensued which ended in decisive victory for the Donnybrook brigade, most holiday-makers being totally unaware of what had happened.

On Monday morning a police sergeant and two constables arrived to inspect the damage and take statements. Nothing came of it. No one had been seriously hurt, and the shattered window was soon replaced. But it was a sign of things to come, and Charlie was one of the first to realise the good old days would soon be coming to an end.

He had already begun making plans for his own clubhouse on the Wing Camp site he had purchased a few years previously, and it was finished early in 1954. At the same time Wing House was being constructed on the plot behind Wing Café, which Dennis and Daphne were now running.

At the end of 1953 Charlie tendered his resignation to brewers Fremlins who tried hard to persuade him to stay. The Rose and Crown was one of their most profitable premises, and they did not want to lose the tenant who had built such a valuable asset.

Charlie remained adamant, and as soon as Wing House was completed at the end of January, he and Bebe, together with Carol and myself, moved 200 yards further east. One of the conditions imposed on his departure from the Rose and Crown, was that he was not permitted to open his new club for a six-month period. He wasn't worried. It was time for a well earned holiday.

Chapter 38
BOMBS AWAY

As it was no more than 25 yards from our new front door to the entrance of Wing Café, I saw much more of Dennis and Daphne than hitherto.

He had become the village electrical repairs man, mending all sorts of appliances from kettles to vacuum cleaners, as well as re-wiring some of the older cottages. It provided useful income while Wing Café, where Daphne was mistress of catering, was becoming established.

On one of my regular trips for a morning cup of coffee he told me the story of the night in 1942 when Minster was "attacked" by the Royal Air Force, and "invaded" by the Home Guard. Dennis and his co-linesmen at the Sheerness Electric Light Company were sent in afterwards to help mop up the debris.

It sounded like a plot the Marx Brothers, or the cast of Dad's Army might have relished, but the night of Tuesday March 31 was no laughing matter for the terrified population of the hilltop village.

Unbeknown to them, and the rest of Sheppey's civilian population, the RAF had devised a plan to prevent German aircraft mining the outer approaches to the Thames Estuary, using small bombs attached to balloons. The theory was that these balloons would be carried by the prevailing westerly wind out towards the North Sea, where they would form an aerial minefield, and be a serious hazard to enemy planes.

To this end the RAF had established five balloon launching sites on each side of the Thames Estuary. On the Essex coastline they ran from Shoeburyness to Frinton-on-Sea, and on the Kentish side from Sheppey to Margate.

This "secret weapon" basically consisted of a yellow-painted canister containing high explosive, attached to a piece of board suspended from a balloon measuring eight feet in diameter. Trailing from the board was a 2000 foot length of piano wire with small drogue parachutes at either end. The balloons were filled with hydrogen, and a fuse, by which its height could be determined, was lit just prior to launching. When the balloon detached itself, the rest of the apparatus slowly descended to form a curtain over the target area. If a plane struck a wire the bomb would detonate, hopefully blowing off a wing or tail plane.

Dennis got an inkling of the March operation when, as a 19 year old apprentice with the SELC, he met an RAF corporal who had newly arrived at the Leysdown camp as part of a balloon squadron. Despite the many posters reminding everyone that "Careless talk costs lives" and urging them to "Keep it under your hat", the corporal told him what they were about to do, and how the balloon bombs worked. Dennis thought no more of it, until he got a close up view of the fiasco that shortly unfolded.

The operation by the RAF Balloon Squadrons, came under the direction of Fighter Command. When the decision was taken to commence launching the balloon bombs the Police were informed, but no one thought to tell the Army Command on Sheppey, or at Shoeburyness.

Sheppey's launch site was on the Lower Road about a mile below Minster village, and there was a strong south-westerly wind when launching commenced around 8.30 pm on a bright moonlit evening. In the next hour and a half some 1300 balloons were sent up, and a further 800 on the other side of the Estuary.

As the balloons gained height they were spotted by a Home Guard unit patrolling near the village. Knowing nothing about the RAF operation, they began firing with rifles at the balloons, thinking they were some kind of enemy ploy. Because of the strength of the wind, many of the balloons rose at an angle considerably less than the vertical, and their trailing wires got snagged on telegraph poles, chimney pots, trees, and anything else that got in the way.

Others exploded prematurely in the air, and more than 200 whose balloons had been shot down by the Home Guard, fell to ground unexploded.

Some balloons burst into flame as the bursting bombs ignited the hydrogen.

The sound of the shooting and exploding bombs sent the population into a panic. Many thought a German invasion had begun, mistaking the balloons for descending parachutists. Then their wildest fears seemed to be confirmed when the power supply failed as a result of trailing piano wire tangling with the bare copper overhead cables.

At first light on April 1, Minster was cordoned off, and the public warned of the dangers of unexploded ordnance. But it was impossible to inform everyone, and there were several civilian, as well as military casualties before, and during the clear up.

Censorship prevented newspaper coverage of the disaster, but three days later the Sheerness Times Guardian mentioned that the monthly meeting of the Sheppey Rural District Council reported that a well known Warden in Minster had been seriously injured while on duty. A week later the paper reported his death.

Some boys and a few adults had narrow escapes while handling unexploded bombs, others were not so lucky, including members of bomb disposal units. On Sheppey a boy and five servicemen were killed, as well as the Air Raid Warden, while three RAF men and two other boys were seriously injured, losing limbs.

In Essex, where most of the balloons drifted inland instead of out to sea, one policeman was killed and two Army men were seriously hurt.

Dennis told me he had picked up piano wire in Minster and the Chequers area for weeks afterwards, but he never saw the RAF corporal again. The Balloon squadron disappeared as quickly as it had arrived. The whole wacky idea was put into mothballs, and never employed again.

Chapter 39
QUALITY LEISURE TIME

Charlie's new clubhouse on Wing Camp was really two large pre-fabricated chalets put together back-to-back, with the interior double wall removed, and replaced by upright load-bearing supports.

It meant that there was a bar at each end of the 70 foot long building, with an area in between fitted with comfortable bench seating and low tables on which to stand drinks and snacks. A passageway down the middle linked both bars, either of which could be shut off from the main section. Outside was a toilet block, and washrooms for the campers.

There was just enough room for two people to serve behind each counter, but that was rarely necessary, for the maximum capacity of the club was only 150. Charlie at one end, and Bebe at the other, were not unduly pressed to maintain a speedy service, and chat to the customers, provided there was someone else around to keep the shelves stocked, replenish the kegs of draught lager, and collect glasses and empty bottles.

I had gained my five GCE "O" Levels the previous summer, and had started my two years in the sixth form. So the pot man's duties fell to a retired pensioner named Harry Burnett, who was the Wing Camp warden, and lived summer and winter in a caravan next to the entrance. Harry did everything from cutting the grass to changing calor gas canisters for holiday makers, and cleaning the toilets. He didn't relish the extra chores of bar work.

When I was at home in the evenings, or during school holidays, he would mysteriously disappear from the area of the clubhouse, and so would I, once I had made sure the bars were well stocked for the morning or evening session. I was legally too young to be a barman, and there were other things in life, like girls.

It was about this time that I had acquired my first regular girl-friend. Her name was Diana, and she lived in Sheerness close to Sheppey United's football ground in St George's Avenue. Her younger brother was in the third form at Borden.

Diana also went to school in Sittingbourne, where she attended the Convent, along with twenty or thirty other girls from the island, who wore the school's distinctive brown and cream uniform. We all travelled on the same trains each day, although I did not know her, until word reached me on the "grapevine" that she would like a date.

I was still naïve enough to believe it was boys who conducted the selection process in these matters, so I did not initially respond. Looks were more important than personality at that age, and I wanted to make sure she did not have pig-tails and braces on her teeth, or worse still ,was a roly-poly.

Discussions with her brother were inconclusive, but I discovered she was slim, with dark hair, that her birthday in March was four days later than mine, and that she was also 16. That seemed a good enough basis on which to begin, so a date was arranged for 7.00 pm the following Saturday evening, outside the Rio cinema in Sheerness Broadway.

I had five shillings in my pocket, comfortably enough for two seats in the 'one and nines' at the rear of the downstairs section, an ice-cream apiece, and a bag of sweets. I remember she was incredibly shy on that first outing, although we held hands in the back row, as we munched our liquorice all- sorts, and the ice-creams I fetched during the interval.

She told me I was her first date, and it became clear that she had succumbed to pressure from classmates who already had boyfriends, and wanted her to be on the same footing. I didn't mind because we got on well, and stayed together for the rest of our schooldays, meeting on the train most mornings and evenings, and going to the Rio, Ritz, or Argosy cinemas on Saturday nights.

After we had turned 18, we often joined the rest of our sixth form friends in having a drink in the True Briton saloon bar, before I would walk her home, and then run down to the High Street to catch the last bus to Leysdown.

We kissed and cuddled our way through musicals like Oklahoma, Guys and Dolls, and Seven Brides for Seven Brothers, Cinemascope epics such as Quo Vadis and The Robe, and of course The Glen Miller Story, as well as countless melodramas and Westerns, the latter when it was my turn to choose.

When Diana left school she went to London to train as a nurse at Guy's Hospital. About the same time I was on my way to Bedfordshire to begin my two years of National Service in the RAF. It was another 25 years before we met again, at a cocktail party for Sports administrators and writers, hosted by her brother at the top of the Martini Tower in London's Haymarket.

Michael D. Britten

We still had something in common, for by then we had both raised three children, and experienced the trauma of a divorce.

Chapter 40
TWO RED CARDS

My two years in the sixth form at Borden were eventful to say the least, both on the football field, and in the classroom.

Towards the end of the autumn term of 1953 the manager of Sittingbourne FC, whose ground was just across Remembrance Avenue, asked me if I was interested in playing for the club in the New Year. He had watched two or three of the Borden first XI's Saturday morning home games from the public side of the school fence.

The School team at that time was better than useful, and we had won all our fixtures so far that term, often by three or four goal margins. For two seasons we had enjoyed regular visits from a qualified Football Association coach, who had schooled us in the push-and-run soccer that Arthur Rowe had introduced so successfully at Tottenham Hotspur at the start of the 1950's. It required a high level of fitness to play it well, but we were young and quick, and had scored nearly 60 goals in 14 matches.

Borden switched to Hockey in the Spring term, when I usually played on Saturdays for one of the teams in the Sheppey League. The only difference was that twice a week evening training on Tuesdays and Thursdays in Sittingbourne meant I would not get home until after 10 pm, after a day at school. I stuck at it, and after a month of circuit training player-manager Arthur Banner asked me if I would like to play in the reserves at Ashford on the first Saturday in February. I jumped at the chance.

Although I didn't score, I gained our side a penalty in a 2-2 draw, and thought I had done reasonably well. So did the manager, and I was picked for the next two matches at Margate and Folkestone, both of which we won.

When I turned up for training the following Tuesday, manager Banner told me he was thinking of giving me a game in the first team in the next home game against Royal Marines Deal. Three of his first team forwards were injured, and a couple of reserves as well.

I could hardly wait to get home to tell Charlie and Bebe, when on Thursday it was confirmed I would be making my first team debut at inside right. I was to partner Frank Neary, Sittingbourne's latest acquisition from the Football League, who had been playing for

Millwall. Neary was a legend in Dockland, not only for his cannonball shooting, but also for his temper. He had a reputation for operating on a very short fuse.

The Bull Ground was packed to its 6,000 capacity when I ran out in the number eight black and red quartered shirt of the 'Brickies', as the town team were called. Neary could see I was nervous, but put an arm on my shoulder, and told me he would look after me.

My instructions were to feed him the ball at every opportunity, either over the top of the left back, or on the ground, on his inside, for Neary to run on to. Twice in the first 20 minutes I did as instructed, and twice Neary blasted two of his 'specials' into the roof of the net.

The next time I received the ball on the halfway line, it came with two Marines as well. It took the magic cold water sponge and a good dose of smelling salts before I got my wind back, and heard my wing partner issuing dire threats to the Deal left half. Expletives deleted, the message was that if he kicked me again, he would have to answer to Frank.

The Marine should have listened. Five minutes later he again clobbered me, and I was carried off on a stretcher by the St John's Ambulance men who were patrolling the touchline. Metatarsals had not been invented then, but I had a stabbing pain in my right instep, and I knew I was in trouble.

The crowd were in uproar, and I swivelled round just in time to see Neary trampling all over the Deal No 6, having floored him with a haymaker. The poor fellow was out cold, and took no further part in the match. Neither did Neary, sent off by a referee, desperately trying to maintain some semblance of control. Our brand new partnership had lasted less than 30 minutes !

There were no substitutes in those days, and I spent the rest of the game as a limping passenger on the right wing of what became a ten-a-side contest.

Despite dunking my right foot in bowls of hot and cold water over the weekend, and a liberal application of arnica, I could barely walk when I went back to school three days later, to be greeted by an irate Headmaster.

He summoned me to his study immediately after morning assembly, and demanded an explanation as he thrust a copy of the local weekly North East Kent Times into my hand. The back page story was all about the game, and in particular the incidents which had seen me carried off, and Neary sent off, for exacting retribution.

The reporter had also done his homework, and discovered that I was a 16 year old sixth former at the grammar school. He further suggested that the Sittingbourne club would be better served by giving more local youths their chance in senior football, rather than employing fading League stars of doubtful temperament.

"You have got to get this football nonsense out of your head" the Head declared. "I will not let you waste your life on something where there is no money. You have a career ahead of you. If it wasn't for that you would be expelled.".

When I protested that I didn't think I had done anything wrong, and I could play for whom I liked on Saturdays, because the school didn't want me for football, he practically threw me out of the door. I had received my first red card. I didn't dare tell him that I had also received £2.50 "expenses", in a little brown packet I had found in one of my shoes.

I later learned that Headmaster Hardy had threatened the Sittingbourne manager with prosecution under the regulations then in force governing poaching of schoolboys. I permit myself a wry smile these days when I read about Premier League clubs offering large sums of money, or exotic holidays, to parents of a promising nine year old, selected to join one of their academies.

In retrospect I should have left school there and then, and followed my own instincts and desires. Football's maximum wage of £20 per week was

Michael D. Britten

lifted in 1961, and my hero Johnny Haynes became the first £100 a week footballer when I was only 24. Instead I stayed at Borden and let Mr Hardy decide what career path I should follow.

Rose and Crown Staff Summer 1952

Public Bar- Bebe, Carol, Author, and Charlie 1952

Donkey Cart (Rose and Crown)

Eastchurch Memorial unveiled 1955

Bristol Brabazon aircraft 1950

Muswell Manor 2009

Rose and Crown 2009

Chapter 41
BLUE EYED BOY

It was another six months before I discovered what career the Headmaster had in mind for me. He had done everything he could to stop me playing football, even to the extent of ordering me to play hockey for Borden on winter Saturdays, but didn't mind for whom I played cricket out of school hours.

When the Kent county club contacted senior schools and asked for their best players to be made available for a trials week, the Head insisted that I took a brand new bat from the school store, together with a new pair of batting gloves, for my net session at Mote Park in Maidstone.

The summer holidays were spent helping Charlie and Bebe at Wing Camp, but when I returned for my final year at Borden, nothing was said about my future until well into November. I was already aware that I would have to do National Service when I left school, and had decided it would be in the Royal Air Force. I still harboured ambitions to be a fighter pilot.

So I was totally unprepared when the Head announced he had entered me for a qualifying exam to New College, Oxford. He had gained his degree there, and in his opinion it would be ideal for me. I would sit the papers in early January, and in the meantime I should decide what I wanted to read, should I succeed in gaining a place.

History was by far my best subject, so that was nominated, and I spent a relaxed Christmas holiday, studying sample exam questions from previous years, to gain an inkling of what was required.

This was the first Christmas and New Year in which the Arnold family was not beholden to other people. Instead of having to work and entertain others, we could all be on the other side of the counter. On December 25th we elected to go to Muswell Manor for traditional Christmas Day drinks.

It had recently been acquired by David Love, and his wife Rene, the younger daughter of our old Rose and Crown neighbours, Alf and Sue Ives.

David was the farmer's son who had inadvertently run over Charles Moore when he stumbled under his tractor outside the Rose and Crown. He and Dennis had become good friends.

Muswell Manor and its cosy bar, with a warming log fire, was the perfect setting for pre-lunch aperitifs, but none of us were really aware at that time how much aviation history had been made close by. There were one or two fading prints on the walls, but nothing resembling the shrine to the pioneers, that has been lovingly created by the present owners Sharon and Terry Munns. Nor was there a commemorative stone, celebrating John Brabazon's first flight. That was not erected until the 90th anniversary of his take off, in 1999.

By the end of the first month of the New Year I had sat the New College exam, the first I had taken in which I was encouraged to express personal views, rather than regurgitate dates and events, parrot fashion. It was a refreshing change, and for once I didn't feel as though I had been through a session of mental torture.

A month later the Head told me the college would like to see me during the Easter holiday. I was to travel up to Oxford, and spent two days there, at the school's expense.

I still chuckle whenever I recall that interview with the New College dons. There were 20 or so, sitting round a very large oval table at which a chair was left vacant for the interviewee. I was by no means shy, but I felt a trifle apprehensive as I sat down and waited for the questions to be fired at me.

I need not have worried. I was first asked how far I could throw the javelin, then how many goals I had scored that season. Then another don enquired whether I knew Colin Cowdrey. I knew of him of course, for he was Kent's finest batsman and was playing for England. But to say I knew him would have been a gross exaggeration, although he had briefly spoken to me at my net session at Maidstone the previous summer.

I suddenly realised what this line of questioning was all about. I had read an article saying that Oxford and Cambridge were worried that they had a preponderance of public school entrants, and were looking to broaden their intake to include more grammar school pupils, especially those with sporting inclinations. Headmaster Hardy must have known this, and had written me up as a combination of Wilson, the amazing athlete of the Wizard comic, and Roy of the Rovers.

Eventually one of the dons asked me which Prime Minister I preferred, Disraeli or Gladstone ? When I answered that I admired the former for his opportunism in purchasing shares in the Suez Canal, but thought the latter would be remembered as the greater statesman because of his genuine efforts to solve the Irish problem, it seemed to meet with general approval, and I was dismissed.

Flights of Inspiration

A month later I received a letter saying that I had been accepted, but that New College did not want to see me until I had completed my National Service. I had a feeling then that it would not be as straightforward as it seemed.

Everyone at school seemed delighted. My form master "Jimmy" Howard said I would be certain to get a Blue for Soccer, and possibly another at Cricket. Even Headmaster Hardy looked as happy as if he had solved a particularly fiendish edition of The Times crossword.

Charlie and Bebe were pleased too, until I applied for a grant to cover the College fees, and was told by the Kent Education Committee that they did not award one to a student whose parents had an income in excess of £800 per annum after tax. Charlie certainly came into that category, but not to the extent that he could afford, or was willing to underwrite my three years at Oxford.

As I had ascertained that the college fees were in the region of £3000 a year, and would be close to £10,000 for the full course, quite apart from living expenses, the only way I would get there was by winning the football pools. Whatever doors a Soccer Blue or a History degree might have opened, were still firmly shut.

Michael D. Britten

I kept my options open until the end of National Service in August 1957, then wrote the letter of regret that I had known for the past two years was inevitable. For better or worse, my destiny was very much in my own hands.

Chapter 42
IN MEMORIAM

A week after I left school the pioneers of aviation returned to Sheppey for the unveiling of a memorial in the centre of Eastchurch village.

Everyone on the island was aware of the ceremony that took place on July 25, 1955, because for weeks it had been featured in the local newspaper, and many had subscribed to an appeal, which had been run by Sheppey resident Wing Commander W.E. James, one of the original naval ratings at Eastchurch.

I cycled the four miles from Leysdown to find a huge crowd had gathered in the High Street and the road to Warden. Every vantage point had been taken, and even the graveyard of All Saints Church was crammed with onlookers, trying to glimpse the semi-circular memorial that had been constructed on the green across the road.

The police had stopped all traffic, but it was impossible to get close enough to see anything, and had it not been for a loudspeaker system relaying the speeches, few of us at the rear would have known what was going on.

The unveiling ceremony was performed by Lord Tedder, Air Chief Marshal of the RAF, who had been deputy to General Eisenhower for Operation Overlord, the invasion of Europe in 1944. Also present were Lord Brabazon of Tara, Sir Francis McClean, and two of the original four Navy pilots whose training he had funded in 1911, Air Chief Marshal Sir Arthur Longmore, and Air Commodore E.L. Gerrard.

Lord Tedder, who had once been commanding officer of the Gunnery School at Eastchurch made a speech extolling the virtues of the pioneers, praising their initiative, courage, and unquenchable spirit of adventure. But it was the address by Lord Brabazon that best captured the significance and emotion of the occasion.

He, uniquely among the dignitaries present, had seen and experienced it all. He had been the first Briton to fly on British soil, and when the first World War arrived, returned to the air, again becoming a pioneer, in the field of aerial photography. He rose to the rank of Lieutenant-Colonel in the Royal Flying Corps and was awarded the Military Cross.

He had been the Member of Parliament for Chatham from 1919-29, and then represented Wallasey from 1931, serving firstly as Minister of Transport, then of Aircraft Production, in Churchill's Government until being ennobled in 1942. Subsequently he presided over a comprehensive study of the future of civil aviation.

Only Frank McClean could boast a comparable record. His patronage had enabled the first Navy flyers to be taught at Eastchurch, and he had been the first to fly a twin-engine biplane. During WW1 he had taken part in regular patrols of the English Channel, and afterwards with the rank of flight lieutenant in the newly-formed RAF, had been an instructor.

He was knighted for services to aviation in 1926, and in the same year was awarded the Royal Aero Club's highest honour, their gold medal. He was twice chairman of that organisation, in 1923-4 and from 1941-44. At the start of WW2 when he was 63, he had joined the RNVR as an adviser with the rank of Lieutenant Commander.

Iona, the youngest of his two daughters, had married Peter, later Lord Carrington, who went on to become Minister of Defence in the Heath Government from 1970-74, and subsequently Secretary-General of NATO.

Brabazon began by outlining the reasons why Sheppey had become the cradle of flying. The first was the decision of the Royal Aero Club to choose Muswell Manor and Shell Beach at Leysdown as their headquarters and aerodrome. The second was the establishment there by the Short brothers of their first workshops.

"British aviation owes a great debt to the Shorts brothers" he declared "one that has not yet been discharged."

He added "Flight in those days was synonymous with the impossible. People who believed in its future, were considered crazy.

"Had they been asked, my colleagues would have said they were producing a system of travel that will bring the world nothing but good. The tragedy is that we produced a juggernaut that nearly destroyed the civilisation of which it was an expression."

"Men were forced to burrow beneath the ground like a rabbit to save their lives from the aerial horror for which we were responsible. As so often happens, technology was ahead of human wisdom. Perhaps that phase is over.

We pray so, and we pray that flight will be used for its rightful purpose. We must do all we can to remove the 'brand of Cain' from flight."

Flights of Inspiration

He concluded : "If we do this, perhaps we may bring peace to the many ghosts that surround us with their misgivings, reassuring and convincing them that by the proper use of flight , all their inspiration and all their toil, and all their sacrifices, shall not have gone in vain, and that as the years go by there will be a realisation of the debt we owe to those pioneers."

Apart from the window dedicated to Charles Rolls and Cecil Grace in All Saints Church, this memorial is the principle evidence that Eastchurch was once an important centre of aviation. The airfield and former RAF station have long since disappeared, and the land is now covered by three prisons, HMPs Standford Hill, Swaleside and Elmley.

The first of these is an "Open" establishment but not to the extent that tourists and aviation enthusiasts are welcome to join the inmates taking a stroll along Rolls Avenue to McClean Walk, Wrights Way, Shorts Prospect and Longmore Drive by way of Airfield View. On the other side of the fence the public thoroughfare linking all three prisons is called Brabazon Road.

In Memoriam. Gordon Bennett!

Chapter 43
THE SINKING OF THE FLYING BOAT

Less than three weeks after the unveiling of the Eastchurch Memorial Frank McClean died at the age of 79. He fully merited his title of "Godfather to Naval Aviation", but Francis Kennedy McClean perhaps deserved even greater renown.

Not only had he funded the instruction of the Navy's first pilots, he had been the financial bedrock of the Short brothers production lines, and also provided land for the Royal Aero Club who were, and remain, responsible for all private and sporting flying in Britain. He might have been the first Briton aloft at Shell Beach, rather than John Brabazon, but for a quirk of fate.

McClean had ordered the first of the six Wright Flyers that Shorts had built under licence, but it never flew because it had been fitted with a motor car engine that was too heavy, and under-powered. Brabazon on the other hand did not have to wait for the second Wright Flyer, which he had ordered, because he already had the Voisin machine he had purchased in France.

The Voisin was used for his historic first flight on May 2, then he further benefited from Shorts' initial mistake. They fitted their second Wright Flyer, reserved for Brabazon, with a Green 60 hp four-cylinder engine, and it was that all-British built aircraft which won him the Daily Mail prize for the first circular mile.

When his flying days were over McClean devoted himself to furthering the prestige of his beloved Royal Aero Club, after being elected to the committee in place of founder member Frank Hedges Butler.

Brabazon had much more varied interests, and made another name for himself in the world of golf in the post-WW2 years. However he is better known in aviation circles for a controversial report in the closing years of the Second World War that had far-reaching consequences. Its repercussions are still being felt today.

When he became Lord Brabazon of Tara, the ancient seat of the Kings of Ireland in County Meath, he was handed a brief by Prime Minister Churchill to construct a blueprint for post-war civilian air travel.

Part of that brief was to draw up specifications for the type of aircraft likely to be needed by British operators after the war. It is important to realise that until, and after the outbreak of hostilities, the aircraft used to maintain links with the Empire were mainly flying boats, such as the Short Empire and Calcutta aircraft, which flew from Southampton Water. They were highly reliable and economically efficient, could carry large loads, and were popular with passengers because of their comfort. Those were not their only virtues. They could take off and land anywhere where there was water, which covered three quarters of the globe. There was no need for expensive land- based airfields.

When Imperial and British Airways Ltd merged to become BOAC in 1939, the new national carrier also used flying boats to ferry supplies and passengers to British colonies in Africa and Asia. One such aircraft was shot down en route to Lisbon in June 1943, resulting in the death of all the passengers, including British matinee film idol Leslie Howard, famous for his performance in the 1939 classic Gone with the Wind.

Yet when the Brabazon committee's list of possible post-war civilian aircraft was made known it did not contain a single flying boat design. The explanation he gave was that his committee could not find an operator who was in favour of flying boats, and that it would have been outside their terms of reference for the committee to insert its own preferences.

That lamentable lack of courage in expressing their own convictions by a group of men of whom the nation had a right to expect better, sealed the fate of the flying boat. Additionally it consigned Britain to the adoption of land-based aircraft produced by the United States. It was another example of the so-called 'special relationship' being to Britain's detriment, rather than its benefit.

Chapter 44
WHITE ELEPHANTS

Aircraft development in the USA had progressed in a very different way to that in Britain. The Americans had no need for flying boats, so they had concentrated on developing land-based aircraft, with the emphasis on transport of both freight and passengers. In Britain the accent was on the production of fighters and bombers. Passenger flight was confined to flying- boats and seaplanes.

These separate areas of aircraft development had been agreed between the two nations during the war, to prevent unnecessary duplication. The RAF top brass had decided that the movement of troops should not be part of their job.

As a consequence, when the war ended the USA had established a big lead in the technology required for civil transport planes, and were poised to take full advantage

Flights of Inspiration

when the days of mass air travel arrived, quicker than had been anticipated.

Lord Brabazon later described this war-time agreement with the Americans "as the biggest mistake in the history of aviation."

The Brabazon committee saw the obvious deficiency and recommended the construction of three types of British aircraft. The first was an enormous Bristol Brabazon with a wing span of 230 feet, to carry over 100 passengers. The second was a smaller jet-propelled version which ultimately became the Comet, and the third was a turbo-prop short-haul aircraft, which after many trials and much tribulation, emerged as the Britannia.

As a gesture to the flying boat lobby sanction was given in 1945 to the construction of three giant Princess flying boats by Saunders-Roe at their Hythe works on Southampton Water. Powered by ten 3,500 hp Bristol Proteus engines, each would have a cruising speed of 385 mph with a range of 3,500 miles in all conditions, and could carry up to 140 passengers in first and tourist class cabins.

These 135 ton monsters never flew commercially, because BOAC trounced the flying boat lobby by declaring they had no interest in bringing them into service. Nor was it interested in the Brabazon 1, the largest British airliner ever made, and the biggest of these white elephants.

This aircraft never had a chance of being economically viable because it was based on the wrong concept. It was constructed in the style of an ocean-going liner, with upper and lower decks containing sleeping accommodation, bars, and lounges. About the only thing it didn't have was a swimming pool!

Brabazon and his committee were trapped in the past, and were not looking ahead. Airline travel between the two wars had been the preserve of the wealthy, and they thought it would continue that way. It never occurred to them that a big plane could carry more people, and thus make the cost of flying much cheaper. So they went for luxury, even including a dining room, cinema, and cocktail bar in their proposals for the Brabazon 1.

Estimates of likely return fares across the Atlantic, ranged from £1,500 to £2,000, an enormous sum in the late 1940's.

Sir Arnold Hall, President of the Royal Aeronautical Society, was later witheringly critical of this British concept of the airliner of the future. He said "We thought it a thing to get in and stay in, rather than a thing to get in and out of as soon as possible."

Flights of Inspiration

The giant Brabazon was envisaged as the flagship of British aviation, plying the Atlantic from London to New York. But only one was built. It had its maiden flight in September 1949, and this prototype logged 400 hours flying time, becoming the star attraction of the annual Farnborough Air Show. Not a single order was received by the Bristol company, and it was broken up for scrap in October 1953.

The Comet jet-liner, made by De Havillands, looked to have enabled Britain to match, or even surpass the American advances, but after a spectacular entrance it faded just as rapidly, following a series of crashes involving considerable loss of life.

The world's first jet passenger service was launched in May 1952 when a BOAC Comet flew to Johannesburg, but within two years the fleet had been grounded. Two crashes in 1954, the first in January 20 minutes after take off from Rome's Ciampino airport, and the second in April near Naples, saw both planes go down at sea with the loss of all on board. Catastrophic metal fatigue had been the cause, and although a much improved version returned in 1958 the damage to the Comet's commercial future was terminal. A fourth version of the plane entered military service as the Nimrod in 1969, and was still in use in the first decade of this Century.

The Douglas DC3 "Dakota" was the American workhorse of the early post-war years, and was widely used all over the world for short-haul flights. Britain's rather tame answer was the Vickers Viking, in reality the offspring of the Wellington bomber.

Having developed the concept of economy passenger travel on their internal routes, the way was clear for American domination of a mass market in which they already had a strong presence with the Lockheed Constellation and Douglas DC4.

In 1954 the first Boeing 707's began to appear, and the following year came the Douglas DC8. If it wished to compete on international airline routes, Britain had no option but to spend millions of precious dollars on buying the bulk of their civil aircraft fleet from the other side of the Atlantic.

Chapter 45
FROM FIRST TO LAST

John Brabazon had always lived life on the edge. He was a devotee of the Cresta Run, and regularly went down the ice at St Moritz until he was 70.

He once said of the experience of hurtling head first at speeds of up to 80 mph : "The Cresta is like a woman with this cynical difference- to love her once is to love her always."

His other great recreational pursuit was the game of golf, which allowed him to occasionally express his love of innovation. Shortly after WW2 he had gone to the USA on a business trip and taken the opportunity to play a round in a brief period of spare time.

One of his American opponents was pulling his clubs on a trolley, instead of carrying them, or employing a caddy. The contraption looked as though it had been adapted from the sort of supermarket cart, with which everyone is now so familiar. They were unknown in Britain, so Brabazon brought one back.

On his next visit to St Andrews to play in the Royal and Ancient club's annual medal he produced the trolley from the boot of his car, stationed his bag of clubs on it, and strode off towards the Swilcan Burn and the first green, seemingly oblivious of the consternation he had caused among a group of caddies hoping for his patronage.

Many of the local men relied on such events for their living. A day's work on the links where a caddy might carry a bag in the morning and afternoon, and receive a good tip if his employer had performed well, would keep his family for a week. If everyone who played the links pulled or pushed a trolley, they would be redundant.

There was much muttering, but nothing came of the incident. It was some time before trolleys became universally used, and even then the expert caddy who could accurately assess the clubs his player should use, and read the lines of putts, would always be in demand.

Brabazon also had a talent for playing the game. When he took it up as a young man, he was so adept that he

Flights of Inspiration

got himself down from novice to scratch handicap in one season. At the age of 69 he was still in single figures.

He was captain of the R and A in 1952-3, and was held in equal system in the world of professional golf. He was elected President of the Professional Golfers Association in 1954, and remained so until his death at the age of 80 in 1964.

That organisation signalled their respect for his tenure of office by naming the Ryder Cup course at The Belfry, Sutton Coldfield after him. The match against the United States was first staged there in 1985, then again in 1989, 1993, and 2002.

Another of his legacies is the English Open Amateur Strokeplay Championship, run by the English Golf Union from their national headquarters at Woodhall Spa in Lincolnshire. Since 1947 the competitors have played annually for the Brabazon Trophy.

He has, of course, his own memorial at Leysdown, where he first flew on May 2, 1909, in the form of a large engraved stone, close to the Muswell Manor house. It was erected to commemorate the 90th anniversary of that flight. He also takes pride of place on the memorial to all the pioneers in the centre of Eastchurch.

Michael D. Britten

And to think I once had the effrontery to suggest that I doubted whether he had ever heard of the place!

Chapter 46
THREE OR FOUR ?

The failure of the aircraft that bore his name was a bitter disappointment to Brabazon. He had been closely involved in both the concept and construction, but personal prestige, flying experience, and his standing as a politician, were no match for market forces, and the overwhelming financial might of the United States. Had it not been for the three billion dollars a war-exhausted Britain received from Marshall Aid, the country would have gone bankrupt. It was in no position to launch a serious challenge in the battle for the airliner market.

Land-based planes were the future, so massive airfields had to be constructed to cater for them. Britain had well over 600 aerodromes at the end of WW2, including Croydon, the old home of Imperial Airways. But that was hopelessly inadequate as the site of London's principal airport of the future. It was not even equipped with radar.

The decision was made to develop the old Great Western Aerodrome, which had been requisitioned by the Air Ministry in 1944, with the intention of turning it into a major transport base for the RAF. Construction of the runways was well under way by the end of 1945, and when the war ended, Heathrow was born.

Gatwick, home to the Surrey Aero Club since the 1920's, had been used by the RAF for flying training, and during the war as a maintenance and repair station. Its grass runways were prone to flooding, but its position alongside the London-Brighton railway line, led to it being upgraded, and opened as a second London Airport, used mainly for charters, in 1958.

Stansted had been a USAAF bomber station from 1942. The Americans had built one of the longest runways in Britain in this hitherto quiet corner of Essex, which returned to RAF control at the end of hostilities. It was the package holiday boom of the 1960's that brought it into use as a charter airport, and from the early 1980's it developed into London's third major air terminus.

It needs only cursory examination of the continuing controversy over the expansion of these three airports, and the widespread talk of building yet another to serve Britain's largest urban conurbation, to realise the far-

Flights of Inspiration

reaching consequences of the Brabazon committee's decision to dispense altogether with flying boats and seaplanes.

Latterly Sheppey has been pitch-forked into the debate because of its position in the Thames Estuary. Boris Johnson, elected Mayor of London in 2008, is an enthusiastic supporter of the construction of a new airport in the area which could easily be connected to the high-speed rail link between the Capital and the Channel Tunnel.

Most of the islanders want nothing to do with it, and point supporters of the proposition towards the former RAF airfield at Manston on the adjacent Isle of Thanet, known since 1989 as the Kent International Airport. It has a ready-made runway, also built by the USAAF, which is capable of catering for the biggest airliners, as well as 700 acres that could be developed in the same way as Stansted was over 20 years ago. It is also within easy reach of the Channel Tunnel rail link.

Those against this idea quote a 1993 Government report that Manston is unsuitable for further development, because of its proximity to the coastal resort of Ramsgate, whose population would be under the glide path.

So what about the 30-40 million people who continue to suffer in similar fashion from their proximity to Heathrow, Gatwick, and Stansted, and the further contamination and transport grid-lock that is likely to follow if one or more are expanded to include extra runways ?

That is the kernel of the argument in this environmentally conscious era. It will need a courageous 21st Century visionary to resolve the issue to the satisfaction of the majority.

Chapter 47
OPPORTUNITY KNOCKS

The future of the Isle of Sheppey also remains problematical. Culturally, it is a paradox. Since July 2006 it has been linked to the mainland and the national motorway network by a handsome £100 million bridge, carrying a four-lane highway over the Swale.

The Sheppey Crossing leads to the island's own "Spaghetti Junction", but that is as far as the modern road system goes. Whether one turns left or right at the former Cowstead Corner, it feeds immediately into narrow urban roads and rural lanes that have scarcely changed for a century.

It is as though one half of the island has embraced the future, and the other has turned its back.

A visitor feels as though he is entering an Edwardian theme park, but one without the elegance and grace that made that era memorable. Nowhere is this feeling more pronounced than in the principal town of Sheerness. A cast-iron clock tower sits at the junction of the Broadway and the High Street, a relic from 1902 when it was built to commemorate the Coronation of Edward VII. Almost every shop looks as though it dates from the same age, and has not been refurbished since.

At the bottom of the High Street where once stood pleasure gardens and a funfair, now stands the ubiquitous Superstore, open 24 hours a day, and slowly strangling the commercial life of the town. When I was last there in the autumn of 2008, there were no less than eight public houses for sale and numerous shops with leases on offer.

Queenborough has the same air of neglect, and the centres of Minster and Eastchurch are similarly unappealing, most of their buildings looking as though they have seen better days.

Yet on the Crossing side of the island there are areas of modern housing and other signs that the island is proving popular with commuters to the industries and better opportunities on the mainland. Young people now have two major advantages that were not available to my generation in the 1950's, namely the motor car, which gives them mobility, and the lap-top computer, which enables them to work at home.

Flights of Inspiration

When the Sheppey Crossing was opened there was renewed talk about it being "a bridge to prosperity". They said the same in 1960 when the one alongside, which carries the railway, was opened to replace the old 19th Century swing bridge. Yet two years later the Dockyard closed and prosperity became a mirage. Other industries shut down and were not replaced, and the loss of the Olau shipping link from Sheerness to Vlissingen in the Netherlands, which operated from 1974-94, was a mortal blow.

Now as 2009 opens there is fresh cause for optimism. The question is whether the islanders have the imagination and will to grasp the opportunities that could lead to enduring prosperity, or will again let them slip away.

Firstly in May 2009, falls the Centenary of John Brabazon's first flight on Britain's first airfield at Leysdown. Every 'swampy' should whole-heartedly support this unique occasion, both in word and deed. Muswell Manor's current owners have organised a programme of celebrations that could plant Sheppey on the map of must-see places of historical interest.

On the horizon are the 2012 London Olympics. There are proposals for Sheerness to become the gateway port for Continental visitors to the Games. Fast cross-Channel boats will bring them to the island, and the Thames will be used as a highway to transfer them to the Olympic site. It is an eminently sensible alternative to adding further congestion to London's security conscious airports, and creaking transport system.

It hardly needs pointing out what future commercial benefits might accrue from a permanent stream of visitors and overseas tourists to the island where aviation history was made. Access to Sheppey is now easy. It is time for all the islanders to indulge in some self-promotion, hang out the bunting, and give the old Edwardian lady a long overdue face-lift.

Author's Personal Details:

Michael Britten is a journalist who was brought up on the Isle of Sheppey, in the village that became the cradle of British aviation. He knows its history, and as a former 'swampy' remains concerned that this corner of the Garden of England continues to be ignored by an ungrateful outside world.

Too little has changed since he left the island to forge a career in Fleet Street, before travelling the world as a freelance golf writer, contributing to many national newspapers and magazines. Currently living in Spain, he has written books on golf and travel. This is his first venture into modern history.

Printed in the United Kingdom by
Lightning Source UK Ltd., Milton Keynes
138545UK00002BA/1/P